THE MIXELLANY GUIDE TO GIN

THE MIXELLANY GUIDE TO
GIN

GERALDINE COATES

MIXELLANY LIMITED

Mixellany books may be purchased for educational, business, or sales promotional use. For information, please write to Mixellany Limited, 13 Bonchurch Road, West Ealing, London W13 9JE United Kingdom or email jared@mixellany.com

First edition

ISBN: 0-9821074-5-5
ISBN 13: 978-0-9821074-5-4

British Library Cataloguing in Publication Data.
A catalogue record for this book is available from the British Library.

CONTENTS

WHAT IS GIN?

Once upon a time, gin could be simply described as clear, unaged ethyl alcohol re-distilled or rectified with a range of berries, herbs, roots and spices, known collectively as the "botanicals". Of these, juniper is the principal flavouring agent. Nowadays, it's slightly more complicated in that, for the first time in 300 years and quite rightly, there is a proper definition of London Gin designed to protect the tradition and craftsmanship attached to the London Dry style. This has given rise in turn to more rigorous definitions of "gin" and "distilled gin". At its most simple this is how they work:

London Gin: Does not have to be made in London, but must be made in a traditional still by re-distilling higher quality than standard neutral alcohol (AKA base spirit) with only natural flavourings (AKA botanicals). No artificial flavourings can be added after distillation. Indeed, the only other substances that can be added after distillation are additional base spirit, water and a small amount of sweetening (not more than 0.5 grammes per litre of finished product). London Gin cannot be coloured. Typical London Gins are Beefeater, Gordon's, Hayman's, Tanqueray and Whitley Neill.

Distilled Gin: Made in a traditional still by re-distilling neutral alcohol in the presence of natural flavourings. Additional natural or artificial flavourings may be added after distillation, as can other approved additives such as colouring. Typical distilled gins are new-wave gins like Hendrick's Gin, the London Gin and Martin Miller's Gin.

Gin: Often known as "cold-compounded", is made from any type of suitable ethyl alcohol (usually a molasses spirit) and does not have to be re-distilled, rather the flavourings are simply stirred into the spirit. The flavourings can be artificial and additional sweetness, colours and other additives are also allowed. In practice no gin aficionado is seriously interested in this type of gin, but it's useful to know about it especially when one is asked why a bottle of supermarket-own label costs half as much as a reputable brand.

THE SPIRIT

The best gins will always bear the description "London Gin" or "Distilled Gin" on the labels. Another sign of quality is the specified use of "100% Grain Spirit". The quality of this spirit is crucial to the final taste of the gin. A clean fresh grain spirit will always makes its presence felt; in fact it is the heart of a properly made gin.

Neutral grain spirit is also the basis for many other iconic spirits. When re-distilled (or rectified), filtered and purified, it becomes vodka. Re-distilled in a pot still and then aged in wood, it's magically transformed into the whisky used in blends. The base spirit used in gin is made in large column stills known as Coffey stills after Aeneas Coffey, a Dublin excise officer. He patented his simple but effective design, in 1831, but in fact his "invention" was an improvement on a continuous still that had been the brainchild of Robert Stein, a Scottish whisky distiller, in 1827. Around this time, designs for continuous stills popped up all over Europe and were soon being exported to the Caribbean and other spirit producing regions.

There are many advantages to continuous distillation: a lighter, cleaner, more consistent spirit can be made in large quantities and the final strength of the spirit can be accurately specified. Importantly, continuous distillation is much more cost effective than having to pass grain alcohol through a pot still several times to achieve the desired result.

Continuous distillation works on a very simple principle, common to all distillation, that water and alcohol boil at different temperatures. When an alcohol-bearing liquid is heated, the alcohol will separate and rise as a vapour, which can then be collected as a liquid. Most continuous stills consist of two linked columns—the analyser and the rectifier. Alcohol bearing liquid in the form of a fermented wash is fed into the top of the rectifier. It runs down, via a pipe, to the bottom of the column and up to the top of the analyser, where it then starts to descend. Meanwhile steam enters the bottom of the analyser and rises slowly up through a series of horizontal perforated plates to heat the cool liquid. As the steam and liquid travel across the plates the alcohol, in vapour form, is separated out. It is then captured in a condenser where it cools and becomes liquid again. The beauty of the system is that the distiller can collect the spirit at whatever strength he wants by adjusting the plates to capture the higher alcohols. In the case of gin, a high-strength, low-flavour spirit is required and so the spirit may be re-distilled until it has become an almost completely flavourless spirit at around 96% ABV.

A curious hangover from the bad old gin days is that, in the UK, the base spirit and the recti-fied spirit—that is, gin—must not be produced in the same location. This is the result of an Act of 1825, one of the many Gin Acts of the late eighteenth and early nineteenth centuries that were intended to control the trade and regulate quality so unscrupulous distillers could no longer make any old rub-bish and re-distill it into gin. As a result, although modern gin distillers often get their neutral grain spirit from sister companies within their huge production empires, Tanqueray and Gordon's Gin, for example, must use grain spirit made at one part of Diageo's Scottish production facility, which is then transported to the other end of the site to be made into gin. Other companies get their spirit from independent producers like the Greenwich Distillery in London.

The new 1825 legislation was a gift to Scottish distillers like the Haigs and Steins. They had first dipped their fingers into gin in 1777, selling around 2,000 gallons of grain spirit to London distillers. Just five years later, this amount had increased to 184,000 gallons and continued to rise throughout the nineteenth century despite protest from English primary dis-tillers. By the 1880s, when the drink trade had industrialised, Scottish distillers using grain from East Anglia and North America, dominated the British spirits trade.

THE BOTANICALS

It's often been claimed that gin is "history in a glass". Nowhere is this more obvious than when one considers the abundance of exotic berries, roots, peels, seeds and barks that are found in a simple tot of our favourite spirit. And it's no coincidence that gin and its Dutch ancestor genever, both flavoured with juniper, spices and herbs, are the national drinks of two great seafaring nations with fleets that travelled the world bringing back strange and colourful foodstuffs from the East and West Indies.

It would be hard to overemphasise how important spices have been in Europe since time immemorial. Frustratingly though, for centuries, even millennia, the trade was almost entirely controlled by Arab and North African middlemen who protected the tortuous routes by which spices travelled from their places of origin in the East. They jealously guarded their sources even inventing fantastic stories such as the one that cassia grew in shallow lakes guarded by fierce winged animals! This sales pitch met with incredulity from the earliest times with Pliny the Elder (AD 23–79) commenting sarcastically: "All these tales…have been evidently invented for the purpose of enhancing the price of these commodities."

In the tenth century, Europe began to get in on the spice action with the powerful city-states Venice and Genoa prospering by importing spices from the Levant and selling them at vast profit in northern and eastern Europe. A war between the two, in 1398, saw Venice victorious, but, whilst everyone knew where the spices grew, for the next hundred years no one could break the Venetian monopoly on the trade routes. Towards the end of the fifteenth century however, European navigational science developed dramatically and it became possible to sail further and further afield. The race was on to get to the spice producing countries and trade directly with them. No wonder when one considers that nutmeg was more valuable than gold and people could pay their rent with pepper. There followed two centuries of exploration, war and invasion all in pursuit of the fabled spices of the Orient. Interestingly, the building of great European colonial empires all over the world was originally a by-product of this activity not its principal cause.

In 1492, the Spanish Royal House funded Christopher Columbus's quest to find a new route to the East by sailing west across the Atlantic. He discovered the New World but died believing he had reached China. Vasco Da Gama, the great Portuguese explorer and navigator, reached India by sailing around the Cape of Good Hope, in 1498, and set up trading posts that allowed Portugal to dominate trade with India for a century. In the early 1600s, the English and the Dutch established their own East India Companies to build a network of outposts all over the Far East to trade in spices and other goods, often using brutal tactics. By the seventeenth century, the Dutch and the English pretty much controlled the spice trade, indeed it was often the cause of war between them. One such skirmish was resolved when England gave Holland the Banda Islands, where nutmeg grew, in return for a minor Dutch possession—Manhattan Island in the New World.

THE BOTANICALS USED IN GIN

The botanicals make gin gin. Each gin recipe has a slightly different botanical mix and, whilst distillers may talk about the botanicals they use, their actual proportions are trade secrets. But we can safely say that all gins will contain juniper, coriander, angelica and citrus in the form of lemon peel and orange peel (some gins, like Tanqueray 10, use fresh citrus fruit). Orris root is also usually an important part of the recipe. Very dry gins often contain a greater proportion of rooty substances such as liquorice and angelica. Whilst there are reputedly over one hundred and twenty botanical ingredients that can be used in gin, most gins confine themselves to no less than four and rarely more than twelve botanicals. There are of course exceptions: more of that later.

Below is a list of the botanicals you are most likely to encounter in gin, starting, of course, with juniper, the queen of them all.

Juniper Berries

The juniper berries found in gin are actually a type of pine cone derived from *Juniperus communis*, a small, coniferous shrub that grows wild throughout the Northern Hemisphere. The berries take three years to ripen and are harvested by beating the branches of each shrub with a stick so that the mature berries fall to the ground to be collected

History has it that juniper berries were the original performance enhancer and it is believed they were used in Greek Olympiads to improve athletes' physical stamina.

leaving the unripe ones to grow further.

Juniper (from the French "*genièvre*") gives gin its name and that instantly recognisable bittersweet taste of pine, lavender and camphor, but the medicinal applications of juniper have been known since the dawn of civilisation. The earliest recorded medicinal use of juniper berries occurs in an Egyptian papyrus dating back to around 1500 BC, in a recipe to cure tapeworm infestations. Juniper berries have been found in Egyptian tombs where they were used as part of the embalming process. They were employed by both the Greeks and the Egyptians to ward off infections and this evolved into a belief, common throughout the Middle Ages, that the vapours from juniper berries could prevent leprosy and the bubonic plague. When the Black Death, a virulent form of bubonic plague, stalked Europe in the fourteenth century, killing over one third of the population, people even wore masks filled with juniper so that its aromas would protect them from the deadly disease. This folk medicine may well be rooted in therapeutic reality as juniper oil is still used in veterinary medicine to prevent fleas. (Oriental rat fleas carried by black rats were the vehicles that spread the bubonic plague.) In humans, oil of juniper is given to alleviate kidney and bladder infections and also to treat indigestion and other digestive disorders.

The juniper used in gin is carefully sourced with the best coming from mountain slopes in Italy and Macedonia. Once at the distillery, the berries are left to mature for anything up to two years until their oil is at its most aromatic. Because each year's crop will be slightly different, distillers will regularly test a number of samples to create the exact blend of berries they require. The proportion of juniper used in gin varies from recipe to recipe. Traditional gins use juniper as the keynote in their recipes and build all the other botanicals around it. In some new-style gins it is barely discernible.

Almond

Almond trees grow all over southern Europe. An important item of trade in the Middle Ages, almond oil is still used in medicines and skin care preparations. The bitter almond, not the

sweet, is used in gin. First ground to release their oil, almonds impart a marzipan like sweetness and softness to gin's complexity.

Angelica Root

According to legend, an angel revealed that angelica could cure the plague and for centuries it was also believed to guard against witchcraft. Almost all gin recipes will include shredded angelica root as not only does it make dry gin dry, it has woody, earthy notes that help to create an integrated botanicals profile.

Angelica Seed

Angelica seeds are widely used in traditional folk and Chinese medicines and are also found in many liqueurs that started life as herbal remedies. In gin, their fragrant, slightly musky notes complement the taste of juniper. Distillers in the past sometimes substituted angelica seeds for juniper when the latter was hard to source particularly because angelica grows wild profusely throughout the UK.

Bergamot Peel

There is an increasing fashion to broaden out the citrus profile in gin by including bergamot peel, derived from the fruit of the bergamot, a fruit mainly grown in Italy. In the eighteenth century, bergamot was used to flavour snuff, gin and, of course, the famous Earl Grey tea, so there is provenance here. Bergamot's musky, perfumed aromas are now found in a number of relatively new gin arrivals (*see* **Gin Brands** *for details*).

Cardamom Pods

The word itself sums up the exoticism of the Far East and, after saffron and vanilla, cardamom is the third most expensive spice in the world. Before distillation, cardamom pods are crushed to allow the full flavour of the little black seeds inside to emerge. Cardamom brings warm, spicy, aromatic flavours to gin.

Cinnamomum Cassia Blume.

Cassia Bark

Cassia bark comes from the cassia tree, which is native to Sri Lanka and China. In flavour and appearance it is very similar to its close cousin, cinnamon, but it is more bitter. Think of Dentyne chewing gum and you'll recognise the taste—sharp and pungent, almost medicinal.

Cinnamon Bark

Another word that conjures up images of faraway tropical places, cinnamon is the bark of cinnamon tree and is generally ground to a fine powder before it enters the still. A pinch goes a long way as its warm, sweet, woody flavours can easily overpower.

Cinnamomum zeylanicum Breyn.

Coriander Seed

Coriander leaves and seeds are an essential ingredient in many Eastern cuisines and its flavour has been prized for centuries. It is believed that the Romans introduced coriander to Britain as a meat preserver and, in the eighteenth century, it was commercially grown in England. Coriander seeds have always made up a crucial part of the gin recipe. They are really tiny fruits that, during distillation, release spicy sage and lemon flavours, and contribute a dry, peppery finish to a well-made gin. Distillers often source their coriander from southern Europe and North Africa but nowadays a lot of coriander for gin comes from India.

Ginger

Ginger is the rhizome of *Zingiber officinale* and is used either in root or powder form in different cuisines and in distilling. Ginger is a staple of Chinese traditional medicine and was mentioned in the writings of Confucius. It was also one of the earliest spices known in

western Europe. Modern day ginger ale and ginger beer have evolved from tavern keepers' nineteenth-century custom of leaving out small containers of ground ginger for people to sprinkle into their beer. In gin it imparts dry spicy flavours.

Lemon Peel

Medicinally prized for its high Vitamin C content, lemon juice was once given daily to sailors serving on Royal Navy ships to prevent scurvy. In gin, dried lemon peel—like other citrus fruit such as orange, lime and grapefruit—adds a crisp, sharp bite that enhances the juniper flavour. Some gins have a stronger citrus profile than others, particularly more traditional gins. But it's rare to find one that does not include citrus in some form.

Liquorice

The root of the liquorice plant is widely used in the treatment of bronchitis and it's a common ingredient in cough medicines. Gin distillers often source their liquorice from the Middle East. It contains sugar, bitter compounds, and a substance that produces a characteristic woody, sweet flavour. Liquorice also softens and rounds out gin's mouthfeel.

Orange Peel

In gin, dried orange peel gives fresh clean citrus notes that provide a counter note to the more pungent botanicals. Some gins, like Beefeater, use the bitter type of orange also known as Seville. Others such as Plymouth use a sweet orange.

Aurantium

Citrus vulgaris Risso

Orris Root

Orris is the rhizome of the iris plant, dried and ground to a fine powder. It is found in talcum powder, perfumes, potpourri

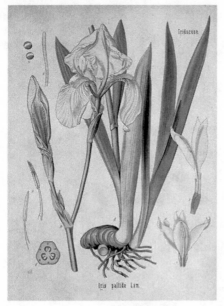

Iris pallida Lim.

mixes and the delicate spice mix—*ras-el-hanout*—used in North African and Lebanese cooking. Aromatic and floral in itself with a hint of Parma violet, in gin, orris acts as fixing agent, holding the volatile elements of the other aromatics together.

MARRYING THE SPIRIT WITH THE BOTANICALS

London Gin and Distilled Gin—henceforth known as premium gin for simplicity's sake—are made by re-distilling the base spirit with botanicals, usually in a copper pot still. Making premium gin is a craft and distillers all have their own ways of doing things.

For many gins, the process starts with charging copper pot stills with neutral grain spirit and adding the botanicals according to the recipe. Spirit and botanicals are then left to steep in the still either overnight or for a full 24 hours. This long, slow process allows for a fuller extraction of flavour from the botanicals and the capture of a wider range of the more volatile oils.

Gordon's, Tanqueray and some other gins are made by the two-shot method where the botanicals are measured into the still in much higher proportions. Once the distillation is complete, additional base spirit is added to achieve the original recipe, a practice that conforms to the new London Gin definition.

Whichever preliminary method is used, actual distillation starts when the stills are gently heated and the botanical-infused spirit begins its journey from liquid to vapour, crosses over the high swan neck of the still and returns to liquid, now gin, in the condenser. A distillation usually takes about 7-8 hours. It's a mysterious process, with each botanical releasing its flavour at different point in the cycle. First come the foreshots, those unwanted elements of the run, that are quickly discarded. Citrus elements emerge, then juniper and coriander, followed by rooty botanicals such as orris, angelica and liquorice. They combine to create a glorious melange of aromas dominated by juniper that fill the stillroom.

The speed at which the still is run is crucial. Too fast and all the flavours bundle up and cross over together in a rush. Too slow and undesirable elements of the spirit are picked up.

The last part of the run through the stills, the feints, is also discarded. Like the foreshots, the feints contain flavours that the distiller doesn't want in his gin. Deciding when to make

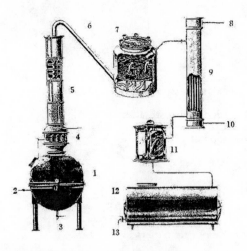

At Greenalls Distillery, where Bombay Sapphire and several other premium gins are made, the "racking" method is employed. Here only the base spirit is put into specially adapted Carterhead stills and the botanicals are contained in a copper basket at the furthest point of the still's neck. The spirit travels through the baskets as a vapour, picking up the various flavours as it goes, so it's a "steaming" rather a "boiling" process.

the "middle cut", as it is called, is probably the distiller's most important job. And, although gin distilleries increasingly resemble intensive-care units with dials and computers softly humming (and it could all be probably done with the click of a mouse), every distiller will taste the liquid coming through the spirit safe until it has the characteristics of the original recipe. Only then is the heart of the gin diverted into the spirit receiver. The point at which this is done is also part of the secret and no two gins are cut at the same time. One can make educated guesses however and it is noticeable that some gins are noticeably richer and heavier. This could be because they contain more rooty substances but also because they may have been allowed to gather heavier elements of the spirit at a later point of the run. Other gins are fresher and lighter because they are more citrus laden and will probably have been cut at a higher strength earlier on.

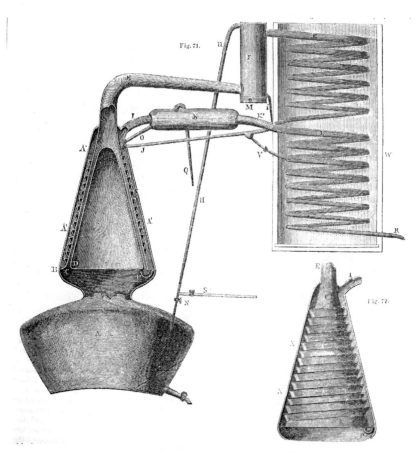

Fig. 71.

Fig. 72.

The shape of the pot still has a major influence on the ultimate flavour of gin as it dictates the speed at which the spirit vaporises and begins to embed the botanical aromas. Most gin stills are copper pot stills, exactly the same as the ones used to make malt whisky. They have elongated swannecks to extract the more fragrant, more volatile elements of the spirit. Many pot stills are characters in their own right such as "Angela" the venerable Madame of the Langley distillery and "No 10" used to make Tanqueray. The still at the Black Friars Distillery in Plymouth has been in place for over 160 years. Its neck is shorter than normal and its lye pipe more sharply curved. No one is inclined to replace it because master distiller Sean Harrison is convinced this design is a major factor in Plymouth Gin's unique taste.

The final stage of production is to reduce the gin to its bottling strength with water. Water comprises around 50% percent of the average bottle of gin and so distillers use filtered, demineralised, exceptionally pure water. Bottling strengths vary considerably with the minimum for all gin set at 37.5% ABV, under EU law, right up to Plymouth Navy Strength's stonking 57% ABV. Most experts agree that for a gin to be considered premium it must be bottled at least 40% ABV. Why, you may ask, when the gin will be served with a mixer or in a cocktail and so diluted considerably? Does it really matter? Yes, because the alcohol carries the complex flavours of the botanicals. Below 40% ABV some of the more volatile citrus elements and aromatic top notes in gin are lost.

TASTING GIN

It's pointless trying to explore a particular gin's character when it has already been made up into a mixed drink or cocktail as most of the subtle flavours will be literally drowned out by the other ingredients. Far better to copy the whisky buffs.

Get some proper nosing glasses as they allow you to swirl the spirit and gather the aromas around the rim where they are more easily detected. Pour a good slosh in so the glass is around a third full. Start by smelling the gin because the tasting process combines aromas detected by the nose with sensory information received on the tongue. Smell is our most acute sense and our noses do the groundwork of identifying individual aromas. (That's why people who have heavy colds complain that they can't taste their food.) Take a good sniff and think about what you're smelling: the aromas most commonly associated with gin are fruit (citrus), floral (orris, rose petals), spice (coriander, ginger, cassia), pine (juniper) and earthy (liquorice, angelica).

Then, reduce the sample to 20% ABV by adding the same amount of water as there is gin in the glass. At this strength the flavours held in the alcohol are released. Water is used because it does not distort flavours.

Traditionally there are only four basic primary tastes: sweet, sour, salty and bitter. (Another one, umami, has been recently added to the list but since it rarely applies to gin, let's keep it simple). Generally these four tastes are detected by taste buds on different parts of the tongue: sweet by the tip of the tongue, sour/acidic on the upper edges, salty at the sides and bitter/dry at the back. So it's important to swirl each gin around your mouth to analyse which part of your tongue is being stimulated.

Here are a few basic guidelines to what we're looking for. Sourness picked up on the upper edges of the tongue indicates larger amounts of citrus in the form of bitter orange or lemon peel. Sweetness is derived from sweet citrus, floral ingredients and from some nuts like nutmeg and almond. Spiciness from coriander is usually detected on the sides of the tongue. A drying sensation on the back of the tongue sometimes indicates strong juniper but can also mean that the gin contains a greater proportion of rooty substances such as angelica and liquorice. And remember, taste is highly subjective: "seaweed in a damp cave on the Isle of Jura" or "a bouquet of summer flowers", for one person, can be a faintly medicinal tang or a cloying sweetness to another.

A gin has complexity when every area of the tongue is stimulated. Texture and body (AKA the "mouth feel") are also important. It's noticeable that some gins are lighter on the palate, others oilier and more viscous. That relates to the botanicals used in the mix, at what stage the gin has been cut during distillation, and its alcohol content. What every distiller is aiming for is balance and smoothness: the alcohol should hold all the flavours of the botanicals in harmony and the botanicals should balance each other.

The finish, too, is another indicator of quality. It's more than just an aftertaste; it's a summary of the whole tasting experience. Ideally, a gin's distinctive flavours should linger smoothly in your mouth after swallowing for a medium to long time, without leaving any unpleasant residue.

DUTCH GENEVER

Gin is a direct descendant of Dutch genever so the quest to trace its roots starts with examining the development of the Dutch national spirit. It's easy to forget that genever or jenever is just as important today in Belgium as it is in modern-day Holland. For centuries, what is now Holland was once part of the Low Countries, a large area of northern Europe that corresponds roughly today to Holland, Belgium and Luxembourg and also included parts of northern France. The region stretched from Dunkirk in the southwest to Schleswig-Holstein in the northeast and was one of the most densely populated areas of Europe. It was bitterly fought over for centuries with the

Holy Roman Empire, Spain and France all vying for control.
These conflicts had a direct effect on the evolution of gin.

THE FIRST
JUNIPER-FLAVOURED
SPIRITS

Although exact dates and written evidence are
sadly missing, most scholars believe that Arab
doctors introduced the art of distilling alcohol
to western Europe, in the ninth century, during the Moorish
occupation of Spain. From there it spread into the monasteries, then the centres of learning and scholarship. In
the eleventh century the Benedictine monks at Salerno in
Italy were famous for distilling spirits together with various
herbs, spices, berries and roots to make medicines. Because
their production methods were written in code no recipes
survive. However, we can be fairly sure that they would have
developed juniper-based compounds to use as a potion since
juniper's healing powers were widely known.

Mediaeval distilling was confined to the monasteries and
the great houses of the nobles all over Europe where a stillatory (a small distillation device) was a standard piece of

kitchen equipment and domestic duties included the production of aromatic cordials and liqueurs to be drunk as
medicinal tonics. Made from a wine spirit, many of them
would have included juniper and recipes for juniper cordials
survive. Evidence that knowledge of juniper had reached the
Low Countries came, in 1269, when Flemish poet Jacob van
Maerlant te Damme wrote about juniper-based medicines in
Der Naturen Bloeme, a natural history encyclopedia. Later,
a proto-gin was invented by Antoine de Bourbon, son of
Henri IV of France. Made from a distilled spirit of wine with
juniper, it became known as "the wine of the poor".

DISTILLING WITH GRAIN

As the knowledge of distilling methods became
more advanced it was realised that spirits could
be made from any substance that would ferment,
not just wine. All over Europe, in the fourteenth and fifteenth
centuries, surplus crops were being used to make drinks that
were consumed for pleasure: in Poland and Russia potatoes,
wheat and rye were used to make vodka; in Scotland and
Ireland whiskies were made from barley.

In Holland and Belgium, genever's birthplace, *brandewijn* meaning "burnt wine" became the catch-all term for all kinds of spirits. Excise records from 1492 indicate that substantial quantities of grain spirit made from local rye were already being produced. In 1582 came the first technical description of grain being used a basis for distilling. In Casper Jansz's *Guide To Distilling, korenbrandewijn* [corn brandy-wine] is described as "in aroma and taste almost the same as brandy-wine" and is "not only named brandy-wine but also drunk and paid for as brandy-wine".

GRAIN MEETS JUNIPER

I n the early 1500s, numerous records exist of the regulations and taxes imposed on distilleries that were making this new-fangled grain spirit. *Brandewijn* was fierce stuff and distillers would have experimented with ways to mask its unpleasant flavours. Dr. Sylvius de la Boe, who was Professor of Medicine at Leiden University from 1658 to 1672, is often credited as being the first to combine juniper and grain spirit in a medicinal drink called "genever". This is most certainly wrong. For a start, his dates are almost a century out. Secondly, it has become increasingly obvious

that no single individual invented genever in the same way that no one person invented vodka or whisky. Medicinal juniper distillates were common throughout Europe at this time and clever distillers quickly realised that juniper and other heavily scented spices combined well with the cheap, locally available *brandewijn* making it palatable. The fact that the new invention was supposed to be good for you was an extra bonus. Certainly looking at Dutch and Flemish paintings of tavern scenes from this time, one has the distinct impression that people are not drinking genever for its health benefits.

What is certain is that genever production very quickly became industrialised.

The oldest Dutch distilling firm still in existence is that of Lucas Bols, which was established by the Bols family, in 1664, in Amsterdam.

In 1672, the van Dale dictionary, the Dutch equivalent of the Oxford English Dictionary, listed a definition for genever spelled with a "g". It seems likely that jenever with a "j" was more common in Flemish parts of the Low Countries.

Between 1500 and 1700, literally hundreds of distilleries sprang up in almost every town all over the Low Countries. In 1602, the Dutch United East Indies Company (the famous Vereenigde Oost-Indische Compagnie or VOC) was established and its fleets sailed the Seven Seas, creating the biggest company in the world with (in its heyday) 50,000 employees. The sailors and officers on VOC ships received daily half-pint rations of genever in pewter cups. They spread the habit of drinking genever to every port and created a huge trade for their national spirit. In fact, genever is proportionately still the most-exported spirit in commercial history. By 1792, the Dutch were selling 4.2 million gallons of genever abroad annually. Shamefully, as the British were to do later, they used genever as a key trading item in the slave trade. To this day, old stone genever bottles are regularly dug up on remote parts of the coast of West Africa—a reminder of that dark period. In parts of Africa, all spirits are still generically known as "gin" even though most of them bear no resemblance to either genever or gin.

HOW GENEVER IS MADE

Even today, the Dutch call genever "liquid bread". A genever distillery looks very like a huge kitchen with the stills resembling enormous cooking pots: The whole is permeated by a yeasty smell like fresh baked bread.

Dutch genever is made in several stages. First, the half product [the base spirit] is made. Nowadays, it can be either a column-distilled molasses or grain spirit, which is then blended with *moutwijn* [maltwine], a grain spirit, made from rye, malted barley and wheat with a fiery taste and a distinctive spirity character. The proportions of half product to maltwine vary according to the style of genever.

Making maltwine (which before the widespread use of the continuous still was the sole spirit used in genever) is still very much a traditional craft akin to making malt whisky. The process starts by pouring a mash of flour and water into giant tubs and adding yeast in order to ferment the liquid. When fermentation is complete, the alcoholic wash is distilled in pot stills a minimum of three times, each time doubling the alcohol content from 12% to 24% and then to between 46% and 48% ABV.

The botanicals used in genever are similar to those used in gin—juniper, coriander, orange and lemon peels, and angelica—but the recipes often contain stronger, more aromatic ingredients such as St John's wort, caraway, aniseed, hops and myrrh. As with gin, every recipe is different and there are different methods of adding the botanicals to the base spirit. Sometimes the botanicals are infused in the neutral spirit for several hours and then re-distilled in a pot still. Or the botanicals can be added to a percentage of the last distillation of maltwine and married with the spirit. Others will combine a percentage of maltwine with a grain or molasses spirit and re-distill the whole with the botanicals. Tradition dictates how different distilleries do it.

There are three styles of genever—oude, jonge and korenwijn—and there are aged and unaged varieties. Under European law each style of genever must contain different minimum percentages of maltwine, botanicals and sugar and be bottled at different alcoholic strengths. This is how it works:

Oude genever is the traditional genever, similar in taste to the original English Genevas. It must contain a minimum of 15% maltwine, no more than 20 grammes of sugar per litre and be bottled at least 35% ABV. It does not have to be aged but often is. It also often has far higher percentages of maltwine than required. Indeed the original form of Moutwijnjenever [maltwine genever] usually has around 50% maltwine but is now quite rare.

The terms "oude" [old] and "jonge" [young] are confusing as one naturally thinks of aged and unaged. But in this case, they refer to "old style" and "new style".

Jonge genever was developed in the 1950s in response to the demand for a more mixable, lighter-flavoured spirit. It is bottled at a minimum of 35% ABV and contains a maximum of 15% maltwine and no more than 10 grammes of sugar per litre. If the label mentions "*graanjenever*" [grain genever], then the base spirit is 100% grain. Jonge genever is colourless and very light on the palate.

Korenwijn (or corenwyn) contains a minimum of 51% maltwine so it has a very malty, full-bodied taste. It must be at least 38% ABV and contain no more than 20 grammes of sugar per litre. Korenwijn is quite rare outside the Benelux countries but if you come across it, it's definitely worth a try. It's the Dutch equivalent of single malt whisky. Drink it ice cold on it's own, or mixed in an Old-Fashioned.

GENEVER INVADES

T he English first encountered genever during the Thirty Years War (1618-48) when the armies of France, England and Spain fought over religion, politics and territory in the Low Countries. Here, English mercenaries were introduced to the local grog, given to steady their nerves before battle. They christened it "Dutch Courage". Later even the great Duke of Marlborough recommended its use "when they were going any time to engage the enemy" and great victories like Blenheim in 1704 and Ramillies in 1706 were credited to genever. When English soldiers and sailors returned to "Blighty" they usually brought their genever habit with them.

However, in 1570, London had become home to 6,000 Flemish Protestant refugees so genever was not unknown in England. Indeed, millions of gallons of Dutch genever were imported to England in the seventeenth century—officially and unofficially—but it was not until the end of the century that the English officially became a nation of spirits drinkers.

GIN'S GLORIOUS REVOLUTION

W hen the Dutch prince, William of Orange, accepted the invitation to accede to the British throne, in 1688, a complete change in English society—not least in its drinking habits—got underway. William was the son-in-law of the unpopular Stuart king, James II. A Protestant, unlike the hapless Catholic James, William was bitterly opposed to everything Catholic and French. One of his first acts as monarch was to declare war on France. Shortly afterwards, in 1690, legislation was introduced to ban the importation of French wine and brandy and to promote the development of home-grown distilling specifically the production of *"good and wholesome brandies, aqua*

The Coat of Arms of the Distillers' Livery Company consists of the sun, with a cloud distilling drops of rain above a double-armed still with a crest, consisting of barley "garbe" wreathed by a vine branch bearing grapes. The arms are flanked by supporters, described in the grant as a "Russe" and an "Indian savage". The "Russian" is thought to represent Baltic rye and barley; the "Indian savage" the source of the exotic botanicals that were imported to Britain from the islands of the East Indies to be mixed with the spirit.

vitae and spirits, drawn and made from malted corn."

The new legislation opened the doors to a distilling free-for-all. Anyone could distil virtually anywhere once a notice of the intention to distil had been publicly displayed for ten days. The industry consisted of "simple distillers" who, actively encouraged to use English corn (meaning any one of wheat, barley, rye and oat grains), made a spirit that was usually harsh and unpalatable. It was generically known as "brandy". They sold this product to the "compound distillers" who, like the Dutch before them, experimented with different flavours to make it drinkable. Very soon, their attentions turned to genever or Geneva, as it was now called. Popular King William and his Dutch court drank it and as a poem in defence of Geneva claimed: "Martial William drank Geneva yet no age could ever boast a braver prince than he…". Geneva was fashionable.

In England, spirits had been distilled since Tudor times but the English had never developed large-scale domestic distilling. There are frequent early mentions of *aqua vitae*, a crude spirit distilled from fermented grain, fruit, wine dregs or old cider. And in 1621, there were almost 200 small businesses in London and Westminster making *aqua vitae* and "other strong and hott waters" for medicinal purposes. Distilling became regulated when, in 1638, Sir Theodore De Mayerne, a physician and alchemist, founded The Company of Distillers. It received a Royal Charter that gave a monopoly to members of the Company to distill spirits and vinegar in London and within a radius of 21 miles. The Company codified the required methods of distillation and the rules governing its practice. This monopoly and the quality standards that accompanied it were swept away in the Distilling Act of 1690 but returned later. Today the Worshipful Company of Distillers is still one of the City of London's most important institutions engaged in protecting distillers' interests and numerous trade and charitable activities.

THE YEARS
OF GIN MADNESS

I n 1689, English distillers produced around 500,000 gallons of *aqua vitae* mostly for medical use. Less than fifty years after deregulation, London produced 20 million gallons of spirits. This figure did not include the vast quantities of illegal spirit as distillers had developed ways to avoid duties by keeping hidden stills and secret tanks. The greater part of this spirit went to make Geneva. Some was properly made in the Dutch style by honest distillers. Most was cheap corn spirit, usually sweetened, sometimes coloured with prune juice and burnt sugar to resemble brandy, and heavily flavoured with juniper-like substances. It was sometimes stirred into warmed ale and sweetened to make a drink called purl , but more often mixed two parts water to one part spirit and sold in quarter-pints in one of London's many dram-shops for the price of a penny as "gin".

A whole book could be written about the years of "gin madness" in eighteenth-century London and indeed there exists an excellent work, *The Much-Lamented Death of Madam Geneva* by Patrick Dillon, which is devoted to the subject. By the 1720s, the streets of London were awash with cheap, noxious spirit. The slums of St Giles were a centre for gin drinking as London's poor discovered this new highly-addictive drug. This area was the setting for William Hogarth's famous engraving, *Gin Lane*, a visual parable on the shocking effects of the gin mania that gripped the city. Here is pictured the slatternly

mother, her legs covered with syphilitic sores, too drunk to notice her child is falling from her arms. Drunkards fight in the street and desperate customers queue at the pawnbrokers in search of money to buy gin. Dangling in the sky is the figure of a bankrupt who has hung himself. Crowds storm Kilman's, the distillers. Carved above the cellar door below is the famous sign: "Drunk for a penny, dead drunk for tuppence, straw for free." Hogarth had been inspired to make this powerful piece of propaganda by statistics such as:

- The death rate in London, in 1723, outstripped the birth rate and remained higher for the next ten years.
- Between 1730 to 1749, 75% of all the children christened in London were buried before the age of five.
- At one point, there were 7,044 licensed gin retailers in a city of 600,000 people, plus thousands more street vendors peddling the deadly spirit.
- Between the years 1740 and 1742, in London, there were two burials to every baptism.
- The hospices and hospitals in the City packed with "increasing multitudes of dropsical and consumptive people arising from the effects of spirituous liquors."
- Nine thousand children in London, in 1751, died of alcohol poisoning.

The whole of London society was scandalised by the story of Judith Dufour, who had taken her two-year-old daughter out from the workhouse for the day, strangled her, and sold her clothes to pay for gin. It was extensively reported in the newspapers of the day and contributed to an image of the London poor as a drunken, out-of-control population. Numerous pamphlets and magazine articles denounced gin as the ruin of family life and slowly the demand for reform became unstoppable.

Attempts began to be made to control the gin madness. They were badly thought out like the one that decreed that only dwelling houses could sell "intoxicating liquors". The Act of 1736 caused the most controversy as it attempted to fix a licence fee of £50 for gin retailers, prohibited the sale of gin in quantities under 2 gallons and taxed gin at £1 per gallon. The reaction was outrage. This Act made Madam Gin the "It Girl" of the summer of 1736, inspiring poetry and pamphlets and even a long-running theatre show written by Henry Fielding, *The Deposing and Death of Queen Gin with the ruin of the Duke of Rum, Marquee de Nantz and the Lord Sugarcane*. Below the Duke of Rum tells how the people reacted to the news that Queen Gin was to be exiled:

RUM:
By different ways their discontent appears:
Some murmur, some lament, some loudly roar,
This day in pomp she takes her leave of all:
Already she has made the tour of Smithfield,
Rag-Fair, Whitechapel and the Clare market: Now
To broad St. Giles she directs her steps.

The play ended with the mob's shout "Liberty, property and Gin forever".

On the actual night before the Act became law there was a night of extreme gin madness. Mock funeral processions

took place all over the country with people carrying effigies of Madam Geneva. In London, taverns painted their punch bowls and signage black and an official funeral for Mother Gin took place in Swallow Street, just off Piccadilly, complete with a horse-drawn funeral carriage and hordes of mourners dressed in black, drinking the last legal gin in copious quantities.

Nothing much changed. In fact, sales of illicit gin— sardonically called "Parliamentary Brandy"—soared, and in 1742 the Act was repealed.

THE GIN OF THE GIN CRAZE

The only thing that modern gin has in common with the gin of the Gin Craze is their shared name. And even that started out as derogatory term—the upper classes' sarcastic description of this new opium of the masses. However gin was a word enthusiastically adopted by its devotees although it had many other nicknames— Madam Geneva, Ladies Delight, Royal Poverty, My Lady's Eye-water, Kill-Grief, Cock-my-Cap, King Theodore of Corsica and Blue Lightning (because habitual gin-drinkers faces often turned blue)—to name just a few.

What were London's slum dwellers drinking and just why was it so detrimental to their health? A recipe from the actually quite respectable firm of Beaufoy, James and Co in Vauxhall gives some idea:

- Oil of vitriol (sulphuric acid): Gave unrectified spirit an extra kick and made it go further .
- Oil of almonds: a cheap flavouring substituted for the coriander and other spices used in Dutch genever.
- Oil of turpentine: used because its piney, resin flavour mimicked the flavour of juniper berries but was much cheaper.

- Spirits of wine: the base spirit, probably not a wine spirit as the first distillation of grain was called "low wines".
- Lump sugar: blended in to disguise the off flavours.
- Lime water: employed for flavour.
- Rose water: incorporated for bouquet.
- Alum: used to make the spirit taste better.
- Salt of Tartar: added as another way to improve the taste of the spirit.

Juniper and other botanicals are conspicuous by their absence. But this distiller was following a quite common practice and it is estimated that, in 1735, approximately five million gallons of gin were made from similar recipes. An interesting footnote here is that Mark Beaufoy, a partner in the business, apparently turned his back on the distilling trade after seeing Hogarth's *Gin Lane*.

In London's slums much worse gin was drunk. The traditional way of purifying spirit by re-distillation was expensive, time consuming and required skill, not to mention proper potstills and distillery equipment. Setting up a distillery could cost as much as £4,000, a staggering sum in those days. The bootleg-distillers in St Giles and the East End needed much quicker results. So sulphuric acid, rock salt and quick lime were used to purify cheap spirit or "low wine" [that is, spirit] that had been distilled once or at the most twice.

They threw in anything else that was lying around and, according to the anti-gin crusaders that often included rotten fruit, urine and animal bones. They stirred in pepper, ginger and other hot ingredients to make the spirit taste stronger and more authentic. Almost certainly they sneaked in hard maltum, a preparation made from *cocculus indicus*, a poisonous alkaloid more commonly employed as a pesticide, which had stupefying effects and was frequently used by nefarious brewers to make beer more inebriating.

At the same time, however, there were reputable distillers plying their craft, making proper Geneva and Hollands, direct copies of the Dutch prototype. Ambrose Cooper's 1757 book, *The Complete Distiller*, was the distiller's bible. One of the most fascinating things found in this manual is the insight it gives into the vast range of natural flavourings then available. With medical science still in its infancy, people relied on natural remedies to cure all manner of ills and Cooper's manual details every conceivable type of fruit, flower, seed, berry and herb that could be used to make "waters" and "cordials" for therapeutic use. He describes the properties of the various plants, what they can heal, when they should be picked and how they should best be stored. His handbook gives numerous recipes and instructions for different drinks including one for Geneva described thus:

Just a few minutes' walk from what is now the busiest shopping district in London's West End was once one of the vilest slums in Europe: St Giles-in-the Fields. The houses in St Giles were called "rookeries" because they consisted of houses and gardens that had been subdivided so much that people were packed into nests. The unfortunates described as "having a cellar in St Giles" were reckoned to have sunk to the very lowest level of poverty. It was a place for the marginalised and destitute and the epicentre of the Gin Craze in the eighteenth century. By 1737, a quarter of the buildings in St Giles were drinking dens. Morning, noon, and night people lay drunk in the gutters of these crowded streets. If you were too poor to afford a glass of the spirit, you could buy a gin-soaked rag to suck. Syphilis, the big health scare at the time, was seen to be associated with gin because women were turning to prostitution to fund their drinking habits. And, although gin was drunk by both sexes, women took to gin like ducks to water and often controlled the street trade. The authorities were very concerned about the ability of these gin-addled women to give birth to and raise healthy children: This was a possible source of the phrase "Mother's Ruin".

Even in Victorian times, when drinking was much more controlled, Charles Dickens described the abundance of gin palaces in this part of London saying "the gin-shops in and near Drury-Lane, Holborn, St Giles's, Covent-garden, and Clare-market, are the handsomest in London. There is more of filth and squalid misery near those great thorough-fares than in any part of this mighty city." St Giles remained a notorious slum well into the nineteenth century until it was finally knocked down to ease the congestion on London streets caused by the arrival of the railways.

"There was formerly kept in the apothecaries shops a distilled spirituous Water of Juniper but the Vulgar being fond of it as a dram, the distillers supplanted the apothecaries and sold it under the name of Geneva. The common sort is not made from juniper berries as it ought to be but from Oil of Turpentine".

Ambrose's recipe is quite different: "for making 10 gallons of Geneva—take of juniper berries three pounds, proof spirit 10 gallons [proof was then equivalent to 51% ABV] water 4 gallons. Draw off by a gentle fire until the feints begin to rise and make up your goods to the strength required with clean water. The Distillers generally call those goods which are made up proof by the name of Royal Geneva; for the common sort is much below proof, ten gallons of spirit being sufficient for fifteen gallons of Geneva".

Geneva was expensive and drunk by the upper classes. Ambrose then goes on to give a description of "what is sold at the alehouses" similar to the recipe of Beaufoy and James and comments wryly: "it is surprising that people should accustom themselves to drinking it for pleasure." He also gives an important clue to the difference between Geneva and Hollands. It's always been believed that they are different names for the same spirit but not according to him. He says the recipe for Hollands is the same as the one for Royal

Geneva but that the distiller "may make a Geneva equal to the Dutch provided it be kept to a proper age." So Geneva is unaged, Hollands is aged.

AN INDUSTRY IS BORN

A fter a number of yet more failed laws, in 1751, Parliament passed the Tippling Act, the first effective control of the production and sale of gin. It was followed by more sensible legislation and increases in tax, which began to drive the bootleggers out of business. The Gin Craze was virtually over by 1757, not least because in that year, and in the following two years, the harvest failed and there was a ban on distilling from grain. By the end of the eighteenth century, cheap rotgut gin had virtually disappeared. Strict controls led to the proper supervision and management of distilling.

London was the centre of the trade and, by 1790, was producing 90% of English gin. As the English city with the biggest population there was never-ending demand. There were also very practical reasons why London became so important to the distilling industry. From its earliest times, the growth and prosperity of London was based on the fact that it had an estuary with a double tide that allowed goods to be brought up the River Thames from the sea into the heart of the city. When reputable gin distilling developed in the late eighteenth century, London's dockyards doubled in size and expanded eastwards. Then London was the biggest and busiest port in the world. Tourists came from all over Europe to gaze at it and marvel at how it was possible to walk from one side of the river to the other on the mass of ships that were moored there.

Thanks to the River Thames, the motorway of its time, London's distillers had easy access to the raw ingredients they needed: oranges, lemons, spices and herbs brought in by the East India Company, sugar from British colonies in the Caribbean; grain brought in from East Anglia and Kent.

There were around 40 distillers, malt distillers and rectifiers, in 1794, in the cities of London and Westminster, and Southwark, according to one contemporary trade directory. Compare this with fifty years earlier when there were reckoned to be 1,500 of them with most owning less than £100 worth of equipment.

LONDON'S DISTILLERS

One of the most important things to realise about early nineteenth-century distillers is that they did not just make a single product as modern distillers do. Surviving price lists and recipes confirm that all of the major distillers made an enormous range of alcoholic drinks, many of which were regarded as restorative tonics. Like James Burrough of Beefeater, they described themselves as distillers of "foreign liqueurs" and distilled anything that could be distilled: liqueurs and cordials from imported French brandy and natural flavourings; fruit gins such as blackcurrant, raspberry, sloe, orange, ginger, lovage and lemon; and bitters, shrubs and punches as well as Geneva, Old Tom gin and eventually Dry Gin.

By this time, the industry had developed into a small number of large malt distillers who produced the primary spirit, which they then sold to a much larger number of smaller distillers, who re-distilled it into products sold under their own names. This may have been because the excise duty only applied to the primary alcohol. The primary distillers were often based in east London and, in the period between 1802 and 1820, they were responsible for between 70% and 80% of all the spirit charged with duty in England.

Distilling had become big business with a number of London trades-people dependent on it for their living. A contemporary account describes them as "coopers, backmakers, coppersmiths, wormmakers, smiths, bricklayers, plumbers, all concerned in the coal trade, all employed on the land producing the corn, landlords, those that carry it to the sea or waterside, captains and masters, sailors, bargemen, corn factors, millers and all those involved in bringing in spices, seeds and sugar from abroad." Farmers, too, relied on the distilling trade as it allowed them to sell surplus- and below-standard grain at a profit. It is estimated that, in the 1820s, around three-quarters of the grain sold in the London corn market was sold to distillers.

Because water is such an important part of the distillation process, many distillers were located in those parts of London that were not only convenient for the River Thames but also close to sources of pure water. Clerkenwell, the site of an ancient and sacred spring called Clerk's Well, was a distilling hub. It was connected directly to the docks via the River Fleet, then the second largest river in London. Booth's was in Clerkenwell probably from around 1740 and had a substantial distillery there by 1778. Nicholson's, once a great name in English distilling, had a large distillery in Clerkenwell. Alexander Gordon moved his business, in 1786, from Southwark to Clerkenwell. Later, in 1832, Charles Tanqueray set up his distillery close to a source of pure spa water further west in Bloomsbury. And James Burrough of Beefeater Gin, in 1863, acquired the Taylor distilling business in Chelsea.

The introduction of a minimum legal still capacity meant that smaller firms who did not have the resources to invest in production were swallowed up by larger firms. Gradually the industry became concentrated into fewer hands. Distilling was a profitable business. It had shaken off its disreputable image and distillers continued to grow in importance and prestige. A major sign of recognition for the trade came when one of their number, Sir Robert Burnett, was made Sheriff, in 1794, of the City of London.

THE RECTIFIER'S CLUB

One reason why the distilling industry had so much influence was that London's distillers joined forces to protect their mutual interests. The Rectifiers' Club was formed, in 1820, and lasted until the late 1840s. Over time, the list of members included all the great names of the London distilling industry, including many that survived until well into the twentieth century and even some that are still around today.

The Rectifiers met once a month in the London Tavern for dinner. According to the Club records, held in the Guildhall library, Mr Gordon placed half a dozen bottles of champagne on the table, in 1837, to celebrate the engagement of his daughter to Mr Edward Tanqueray. Within this bonhomie and socialising, a lot of hard business was accomplished: for example, agreeing to fix the prices of gin, bitters, cordials and liqueurs amongst themselves. As is the way of these things, the next meeting recorded complaints that some members were underselling contrary to the agreement. Rises in the price of spirits, due to ever increasing taxation, was a common subject of debate. The Rectifiers wrote a joint letter, in March of 1825, to the Chancellor of the Exchequer, asking him to bring forward his proposed reduction of duty on spirit as they "are suffering a great stagnation of sales" and want "a revival in demand." Amazingly, the Chancellor agreed.

It seems clear that London's distillers were a very tight-knit group, many related to each other, marrying into each other's families and very able to act as one to defend the interest of their trade. One could almost describe them as a mafia.

OLD TOM GIN

At the beginning of the nineteenth century, the gin sold in barrels to retailers was often accompanied by descriptors such as "Old Tom", "Young Tom", "Celebrated Cream Gin", "Cream of the Valley" and "Out and Out". What seemed to have happened over time was that, in much the same way, as Hoover became the common name for any type of vacuum cleaner, Old Tom became the generic name for gin and later evolved into the term distillers used for sweetened gin. In the beginning, however, all gin was sweetened: first, because sugar very effectively masked fusel oil flavours in the base spirit before the invention of the continuous still allowed a clean neutral spirit to be made; secondly, because popular taste leant toward sweetness. Old Tom was then produced around 25% ABV and was sold in drams in the gin palaces to be drunk neat like a liqueur.

In taste terms, Old Tom gin is often described as the missing link between Dutch genever and modern Dry gin.

An existing example of the style reveals a richer, maltier spirit akin to new-make spirit, and a distinct sweetness. The quality of Old Tom gin would have varied greatly and, as with modern gins, each distiller would have had his own recipe. Some Old Toms would have been like a cordial or liqueur— heavily sweetened with sugar and glycerine and strongly flavoured with juniper and other herbs—often described as "cordial gin". But most distillers simply added sugar to their recipes for Old Tom gin. An original 1864 recipe for Dry and Old Tom gin found in the Beefeater Distillery lists juniper berries, coriander seed, angelica root, ground liquorice root and winter savoury. This is a valuable document as it strongly indicates that many distillers used the same combination of botanicals for both Dry and Old Tom gins but added sugar to the Old Tom version. Here, the proportions for Old Tom are specified as 40 pounds of loaf sugar for every 100 gallons of spirit. A few distillers didn't use sugar at all but instead employed botanicals like liquorice and sweet fennel to achieve a musky sweetness.

As distilling techniques advanced, the quality of the spirit dramatically improved but this sweetened gin was still popular so distillers continued to make it and, in fact, charge more for it than for Dry Gin.

It is believed that Old Tom gin got its name from a certain Captain Dudley Bradstreet, an enterprising bootlegger.

When the first spectacularly unsuccessful attempt to control gin sales was made in 1736, he acquired a property on Blue Anchor Lane and invested £13 in gin purchased from Langdale's distillery in Holborn. He set up a painted sign of a cat in the window and broadcast the fact that gin could be purchased "by the cat". Under the cat's paw sign there was a slot and a lead pipe, which was attached to a funnel situated inside the house. Customers placed their money in the slot and duly received their gin. Bradstreet's business prospered until complaints about the "cat-man" became too numerous and competitors emerged. His idea was soon copied all over St Giles where people would stand outside houses, call out "puss" and when the voice within replied "mew", they knew that they could buy bootleg gin inside. By the middle of the eighteenth century, Old Tom was the street name for gin.

Old Tom gin remained fashionable until the turn of the century and many cocktail recipes from this period specify it in such drinks as the Martinez and the Tom Collins. In fact, many cocktail books right up until the 1950s, such as David Embury's *The Fine Art of Mixing Drinks*, claim that a Tom Collins can only be made with Old Tom gin.

Old Tom and Dry gin existed side by side until the turn of the century but then gradually Dry gin began to edge out Old Tom because the taste for very sweet drinks waned. Old Tom gin continued to be made in Plymouth and Warrington and by all the major London firms until around the 1960s when, because of lack of demand, production slowly ceased. Old Tom then became virtually extinct but it's become available again as a number of Old Tom-style gins have launched in response to modern bartenders' desire to create the authentic cocktails of yester year. (*see* **Brands** *for details*)

THE RISE
OF LONDON DRY

T hroughout the early nineteenth century, when people drank gin, they were usually drinking Old Tom, Geneva or Hollands. But by the 1850s, something else was happening too, and that was the gradual displacement of heavy, sweet gin by unsweetened, clear gin. It came to be known as the London Dry style. "Dry" because it was unsweetened— or as distillers liked to advertise it—"sugar free gin." "London" because most of the distillers making it were based in London.

There are several reasons why this new style of gin gradually took over. First, of course, was the widespread use of the continuous still that allowed a purer, more consistent spirit to be cost-effectively made. Now the quality of a pure grain spirit could be enhanced with more subtle flavours rather than disguised with sugar and heavy aromatics. Secondly, a great disaster overtook London's distillers, in the 1870s, when the impact of the dreaded phylloxera blight began to be felt. Phylloxera was an aphid infestation imported on vine stock shipped from the US to France, in 1862, which destroyed most of Europe's vineyards. Consequently, brandy became almost unobtainable.

Let's not forget that all distillers then made a huge variety of liqueurs using French brandy. Cherry brandy, curaçaos, parfait amour, ginger brandy, maraschino, noyeau and others were the big sellers. Suddenly an entire income stream disappeared. Distillers realised that they had to diversify and many of them began to bottle Scotch and Irish whiskies as "British liqueurs". They also began to look at gin with new eyes as the upper classes, now deprived of brandy, drank gin in greater quantities and wanted a more sophisticated spirit. One only has to look at the stock lists of distillers like Beefeater's founder James Burrough to see that, from 1876, there was an increasing emphasis on gin, now sold under brand names such as Ye Old Chelsey, Black Cat Gin, James Burrough London Dry and Old Tom Gins and even an aged Fine Old Malt Gin. Other distillers took the same route, not least of which because slowly but surely gin had

A piece of correspondence still exists that took place between Charles Dickens and the gin distiller Seager Evans, concerning Dickens' order of Old Tom gin which had duly arrived. The author complained that it was adulterated and tactfully blamed that on the railway workers who had transported it.

crawled out of the gutter to become a drink for the affluent middle classes.

Despite another minor gin panic, in the 1830s, attitudes toward drink and drinking fundamentally changed during Queen Victoria's long reign. The arrival of the gin palaces intro-duced the idea of drinking as a social activity, part of daily life. The first to open in London was probably that of Thompson & Fearon's in Holborn in around 1832. Whilst many disap-proved, the gin palaces were the last word in luxury and glamour, a place where ordinary people could escape the drudgery of work and the mean-ness of their surroundings. Dickens describes them, in *Sketches by Boz*, in Hemingway-esque terms:

> "You turn the corner. What a change. All is
> light and brilliancy. The hum of many voices
> issues from that splendid gin-shop which
> forms the commencement of the two streets
> opposite; and the gay building with the fan-
> tastically ornamented parapet, the illuminated
> clock, the plate-glass windows surrounded by
> stucco rosettes, and its profusion of gas-lights

in richly-gilt burners, is perfectly dazzling when contrasted with the dirt and dark we have just left. The interior is even gayer than the exterior. A bar of French-polished mahogany, elegantly-carved, extends the whole width of the place; and there are two side-aisles of great casks, painted green and gold, and bearing such inscriptions as 'Old Tom, 549'; 'Young Tom, 360'; 'Samson, 1421' the figures agreeing, we presume, with 'gallons' understand. Beyond the bar is a lofty and spacious saloon, full of the same enticing vessels, with a gallery running round it, equally well furnished. On the counter, in addition to the usual spirit apparatus, are two or three little baskets of cakes and biscuits which are carefully secured at the top with wicker-work to prevent their contents being unlawfully extracted".

Gin palaces were quite different to the rackety gin she-beens of the past and some of their glamour rubbed off on gin itself.

The suspension of excise duties on gin in bond for export, in 1850, opened up new markets for gin and it was soon an important export earning money for the Treasury and boosting Britain's worldwide reputation as the source of everything excellent. The trade had been kick started by the Royal Navy. In the early nineteenth century, gin became the drink of officers on Navy ships and wherever the Navy went, gin went too. (The connection between gin and the Navy remains in the "gin pennant," the green and white flag traditionally run up as an invitation to board.) Requests for London and Plymouth Gin poured in from every corner of the world with Gordon's for example sending a shipment to a group of Australian miners who paid in gold dust.

This was also the great age of colonialisation when the sun never set on the British Empire. For thousands of expats serving in far-flung outposts English gin was not just a cure for homesickness, it was a life saver, literally. They drank it with another new invention—tonic water—to prevent malaria. When they finally came home to the Home Counties they brought the taste for this new, sophisticated drink with them.

Genteel Victorian women bought the new-style gin in grocery shops thanks to a law of 1861 that allowed shops to retail spirits. They served gin at tea parties from decanters labelled "Nig" in a bourgeois attempt to confuse the servants and called it "white wine". By this time, the fashion for "banting" or slimming was in full swing and people had begun to realise the danger of indulging in sugar and starch. Tastes changed, veering away from sweet to more subtle flavours and distillers began to advertise their gin as being "sugar-free".

English distillers began to sell gin, in the 1880s, in proprietary bottles to cater for the off-licence trade. Up until then gin had been sold in barrels and the retailers would put it into containers for their customers to take home. The first gin bottles were dark green and heart shaped, straight copies of Dutch genever bottles. Later bottles were made of clear glass because export customers wanted to see exactly what they had purchased. (Domestic Gordon's Gin is still sold in dark green bottles and export gin in clear, a throwback to this practice). Soon sophisticated packaging and advertising promoted London Dry Gin as a quality product both at home and abroad.

Joseph Boord was the first distiller to use an image of a cat on his 1849 Cat-and-Barrel trademark for his Old Tom gin. It's one of the earliest known trademarks for gin and also appeared on labels for the company's liqueurs and Dry gins. At this time, all the big distilling firms sold Old Tom gin and once branded bottles came in, the packaging invariably carried an image of a tomcat. The Boord Company maintained production throughout the Second World War and, in 1963, was taken over by Booth's. The firm was dissolved in 1993.

'A FINE SPIRIT

There's a fine spirit about when you've got some Boord's London Gin. This famous brand is always recognised by the Cat and Barrel label.

NICHOLAS TRATARIS
P.O. Box 58, BLANTYRE

BOORD'S FINEST LONDON GIN

GIN COMES INTO ITS OWN

O ne reason for the new Dry gin's success is that it was more mixable than the heavier style. Cocktails first arrived in Europe, in the 1860s, brought over by Americans who imported the fashion for sweet mixed drinks. American style cocktails differed from Victorian drinks such as cups, punches, toddies, flips, fizzes, daisies, cobblers and slings, in that they were heavily iced.

The establishment of the Wenham Lake Ice Company in the Strand in 1845 made ice commercially available in London for the first time. The first American cocktail bar opened, in the 1860s, behind the Bank of England and soon cocktail bars popped up all over London. The Criterion in Piccadilly opened in 1870 and grand hotels like the Savoy and Claridge's boasted the inclusion of American bars with a wide range of cocktails based on gin. Some Londoners disapproved. And in 1863, Henry Porter and George Rob-

THE
WENHAM LAKE ICE COMPANY,
125, STRAND, LONDON.
Established 1845.

ICE SAFES.

The NEW DUPLEX REFRIGERATOR. Registered.
So arranged that either Wenham Lake or Rough Ice may be used to C.
PRIZE MEDAL REFRIGERATORS. 1851 and 1862.
Fitted with Water Tanks and Filters, and all real Improvements.
The New American DOUBLE-WALL ICE-WATER-
PITCHER. Safe for Cooling Cups, Iced Water, &c.
The   BUTTER DISH, with Revolving Lid,

Illustrated Price Lists Free on application.

WENHAM LAKE ICE COMPANY,

erts expressed their opinion in print: "for the sensation drinks which have lately travelled across the Atlantic we have no friendly feeling ...we will pass the American Bar...and express our gratification at the slight success which 'Pick-me-up', and Corpse Reviver" have had in this country". However Mrs Isabella Beeton, the domestic goddess of Victorian England, begged to disagree and included recipes for Mint Juleps and Gin Slings in her famous 1861 edition of *Book of Household Management*.

Cocktails caught on and cocktail books featuring gin recipes were widely published. Jerry "the Professor" Thomas's 1862 *The Bar-Tender's Guide and Bon Vivant's Companion* appeared. He toured Europe, in 1859, with his own travelling bar giving demonstrations and many European bartenders came to learn from the master. Harry Johnson's 1882 book, *Bartender's Manual or How to Mix Drinks of the Present Style*, became another bestseller.

A very vociferous Temperance movement had officially got underway, in 1832, at a mass rally in Preston, Lancashire with the signing of the first pledges to abstain from alcohol. Despite all the efforts of the British prohibitionists, their major achievement was to establish the right to drink in British law, as evidenced by the bishop who firmly declared during a licensing debate in the House of Lords: "I would rather see England free than England sober." At the General Election of 1874, the Liberal Government was rejected by voters, angry at Gladstone's kow-towing to the prohibitionists. Gladstone wrote, "We have been borne down in a torrent of gin...."

In the United States, imported English Dry gin and Old Tom gin were sold in equal amounts until the 1890s, but from then on Dry gin became the preferred cocktail spirit. There,

the Dry Martini and the Bronx—both dry gin drinks—were
the most popular cocktails.

PROHIBITION

On January 17th 1920, the Volstead Act passed
through the US Congress and Prohibition came
into force. It soon turned into a re-enactment
of the eighteenth century Gin Craze as millions of ordinary
Americans turned into amateur distillers and professional
drinkers. A popular song summed up the mood:

> *Mother makes brandy from cherries*
> *Pop distils whisky and gin;*
> *Sister sells wine from the grapes on our vine—*
> *Good grief how the money rolls in*

Organised crime quickly moved in on illicit alcohol man-
ufacture and smuggling as there were vast profits to be made.
An entire generation of Americans became criminals in
one form or another either by going to speakeasies to drink,
distilling at home or buying bootleg booze. Not exactly the
scenario envisaged when many US towns closed down their
jails on the eve of Prohibition in the anticipation that, once
alcohol was banned, there would be no more crime.

Bathtub gin was popular. It was a vile combination of industrial alcohol, glycerine and juniper oil made in such large containers that water was added by the bath tap. To make it taste better people added fruit juices, mixers and bitters inventing a raft of new cocktails.

English distillers had feared losing their most important export market as a result of Prohibition. In fact, the reputation of imported English gin reached new heights as, having experienced the effects of truly bad moonshine, people were ready to pay exorbitant sums for the real stuff. It is estimated that, during Prohibition, London distilleries exported around 40 million dollars worth of gin to the US via Canada, the West Indies and islands close to American shores. No questions were asked when requests came in that orders should be packaged so that they could float.

As early as the 1890s, most English distillers were producing proprietary ready mixed cocktails often in bottles shaped like cocktail shakers.

On the 5th December 1933, the "noble experiment" ended and America re-entered the civilised world.

DRY GIN RULES SUPREME

The 1920s and 1930s were gin's glory days. It was the age of glamour, an explosion of the new in technology, music, fashion, the arts and popular culture. Along with fast cars, short skirts, bobbed hair, modern art, cinema and jazz, drinking cocktails was the height of fashion.

London of the 1920s saw the arrival of many of America's leading barmen and cocktail experts who had come in search of work, driven from home by Prohibition. By now gin cocktails were simpler and new, sophisticated drinks such as the Clover Club and the White Lady were lapped up by high society in cocktail bars like Ciro's Club and the American Bar at the Savoy.

The writer Evelyn Waugh described the racy lives of young moneyed aristocrats in novels and christened them the "Bright Young Things". Newspapers and magazines were fascinated by everything this smart set did, the first glimmerings of the modern obsession with celebrity. They were a distraction from the economic depression and mass unemployment of the years between the two World Wars, a time when the old formal social order began to disappear.

Cocktail parties became the rage, copying the American fashion of replacing the British custom of afternoon tea with early evening cocktails in grand hotels. Dressing up for formal dinners had been abandoned and the cocktail hour was the perfect way to fill the vacuum, creating another opportunity for frantic socialising.

And gin was the spur for this manic pace of life. In Noël Coward's 1926 stage play *Words and Music*, the debutantes sing:

> "*The Gin is lasting out*
> *No matter whose*
> *We're merely casting out*
> *The Blues.*
> *For Gin in Cruel*
> *Sober Truth*
> *Supplies the Fuel*
> *For Flaming Youth*".

Riding the cocktail zeitgeist, distillers became much more sophisticated in their marketing. "Drinks never taste thin with Gordon's Gin" was the strapline for Gordon's advertising. At this time, Plymouth Gin and Booth's Gin were the two most famous gin brands in the world and both invested heavily in promoting their products. Booth's Gin published *An Anthology of Cocktails* in the 1930s, which featured the favourite cocktails of society figures, and heart throbs such as silent-screen idol Ivor Novello.

Further down the social scale gin was "in", too. Cocktails never invaded the pub where the most popular mixers for gin were bitters, orange squash, ginger beer, peppermint and lime cordials and, of course, tonic water. A perennial favourite in working men's pubs was the Dog's Nose—a glass of gin poured into a pint of beer.

GIN NOW

During the Second World War, all distilling from grain was prohibited in order to conserve stocks of grain for food and most distilled alcohol was diverted to the war effort —described by the stoical British as "Cocktails for Hitler". However, despite rationing, some gin was still made for the domestic market, using a molasses spirit. Once the war was over, English distillers were back in action, building huge export trades and making imported English-made gin the world's most sophisticated spirit.

Gin remained the dominant white spirit right up until the early 1960s, a time when probably around half of any cocktail list would be made up of gin based drinks. Gin was glamorous: to this day the last take of every Hollywood movie is still called the "Martini shot" as that was the signal for everyone, from big name star to the guy who holds the clapper board, to celebrate in style with Martinis—Gin Martinis. Then came vodka. By the 1970s, gin was almost stagnant in terms of growth. Many traditional brands simply disappeared. Even worse, gin lost its iconic image and was perceived as the opposite of "cool", a drink your parents drank.

Times change and gin is once more the star of the scene. Its revival began, in 1988, when Bombay Sapphire launched. Stylish packaging and a less juniper-dominated taste profile attracted a whole new audience for gin and Bombay Sapphire proved it was possible to re-invent the category. Its success was the catalyst for a wave of activity and a host of new, unusually-flavoured gins have emerged and are still emerging.

The 1990s cocktail renaissance also put gin firmly back in the spotlight. No two gins taste quite the same and high-quality gins with interesting new flavours inspire bartenders to come up with drinks that showcase gin's unique personality as well as different brands' specific botanical recipes. At the same time, there's been a revival of interest in the traditional brands and classic cocktails. Gin, a spirit with flavour, heritage and provenance, is now back—big time.

GIN BRANDS

The brands reviewed here are alphabetically arranged. With very few exceptions they are all premium gins, bottled at above 40% ABV. Or they are brands with an interesting history. This is by no means a comprehensive list. And although UK made gins dominate, the best US, French and Spanish gins are also included. All are widely available either in retail or on drinks' internet sites.

Aviation

In the US, microdistilling, like microbrewing before it, has taken off and there are currently around 90 craft distilleries. In 1990, there were five. American microdistillers have tapped into the backlash against mass-produced products and experiment with a range of premium small-batch spirits. Increasingly, it's gin. Reinventing the London Dry formula, they push exotic citrus and aromatic ingredients to the forefront and let juniper take a back seat. Aviation Gin is typical of this style. It's a collaboration between House Spirits Distilling in Portland, Oregon and mixologist Ryan Magarian and was made with the Aviation cocktail in mind. Botanicals in the mix are juniper, cardamom, coriander, lavender, anise seed, sarsaparilla, and dried orange peel. Re-distilled with a 100% rye-grain neutral spirit and bottled at 42% ABV there are strong hints of Dutch jonge genever. Aviation is the ideal base for the many citrus-based vintage gin cocktails that are back in fashion again.

Beefeater Dry

James Burrough, the founder of Beefeater Gin, was born in Devon in 1835. He trained as a pharmacist in Exeter before setting off to seek his fortune in North America. Five years later James returned to the UK in search of his next commercial opportunity. That was the Chelsea distilling and rectifying firm of John Taylor, established in 1820, which James purchased, in 1863, for £400.

Taylor specialised in the production of liqueurs, fruit gins, gin and punches. It had an excellent reputation and loyal customers such as Fortnum and Mason. James took over the business renaming it "James Burrough, Distiller and Importer of Foreign Liqueurs". He used his knowledge of science to perfect his recipes. The business did well and, in 1871, James began to improve and extend the distillery buildings.

When the phylloxera blight struck European vineyards, James turned his attention to the domestic spirit that would benefit enormously from the ensuing brandy shortage—English gin. A notebook, from 1879, shows that James constantly experimented with different proportions of orange in his gin recipe, perhaps because he had found a reliable supplier in Covent Garden and the orange-based liqueurs were his most successful.

Beefeater is an exceptionally clean, bold gin whose extravagant juniper character is balanced with very strong citrus. On the nose juniper is dominant whilst in the mouth the full-bodied aromatic character of the gin emerges, to be followed by a long and complex finish. Still made to James Burrough's original recipe, it contains juniper, coriander, Seville orange peel, lemon peel, almond, angelica root and seed and liquorice, Beefeater owes its distinctively clean taste to the fact that it is based on a pure grain spirit. Another reason for Beefeater's rich character could be the fact that it is made by the steeping method, where the botanicals are steeped in the grain spirit for 24 hours before being gently heated and allowed to run through the still. The final spirit is reduced to 40% ABV.

Beefeater is the only London Dry gin from the glory days when London-made gin dominated, that is still made in London at its distillery in Kennington—a cricket ball's throw away from the famous Oval cricketing ground. Beefeater has always had a major export trade thanks to its early positioning as a characteristically "English" product. That tradition continues: Beefeater is still a leading brand in over 170 countries around the world.

Beefeater 24

Beefeater 24 is the luxury super-premium addition to the Beefeater Gin portfolio launched in October 2008. Like Beefeater Dry, Beefeater 24 is made in the heart of London. Like Dry, too, it's made by the steeping method.

Master distiller Desmond Payne has applied his years of experience to the creation of 24. Having long been fascinated by the potential of tea in the botanicals mix he was delighted to discover that the father of James Burrough had been a tea merchant in London, supplying fine teas by Royal

Appointment to Queen Victoria. Building on this historic link, Payne's voyage of discovery began. After almost two years of constant experimentation, the recipe was complete. It includes the core botanicals that define the distinctive, instantly recognisable Beefeater taste—juniper, coriander, angelica root and seed, almond, Seville orange peel, lemon peel, orris and liquorice. To these are added a unique blend of Chinese green and rare Japanese Sencha teas and a citrus boost in the form of grapefruit peel. The spirit is "cut" at an earlier stage and a smaller percentage of the run is taken in order to retain the fresher, more volatile flavours of grapefruit and the leaf teas. On the nose, notes of citrus, juniper and the aromatic scent of Sencha are immediately apparent. In the mouth, there's a burst of citrus followed by juniper developing into a long finish with spicy coriander balanced by the dryness of angelica and the woodiness of liquorice. Beefeater 24 is a London Dry Gin, which means that no colouring or flavour has been added after distillation. Bottled at 45% ABV, it's a glamorous, sophisticated spirit that has motivated some of the world's top mixologists to come up with stunning new cocktails.

Berkeley Square

Berkeley Square is the new premium gin from master distillers G & J Greenall that is inspired by the herbs of an English physic garden. To the core botanicals of juniper, coriander, angelica and cubebs is added basil, sage, lavender and citrus in the form of kaffir lime leaves. It is made in a two-day process using a *bouquet garni* technique. First, the core botanicals and the kaffir lime leaves are placed in a copper pot still filled with triple-distilled grain spirit, which is left to macerate for a day. The other botanicals are then wrapped in muslin and steeped in the spirit to infuse their oils. On the second day, the still is run very slowly and gently to pick up the delicate essential oils of the *bouquet garni*.

Whilst it's not at its best in a G & T, the green herbaceous botanicals in Berkeley Square make it an ideal gin to experiment with for interesting and delicious herbal cocktails

Bluecoat Gin

Named after the blue uniforms of the American militia in the Revolution, this Philadelphia-made gin describes itself as an American Dry Gin, a far better name than the attempts to designate new style US gins as

'New Western Dry". The differentiating feature of Blue-coat is the use of organic juniper and citrus in a neutral grain spirit made from rye, wheat, barley and corn that is then filtered before bottling at 47% ABV. Batch distilled over a long, slow 10-hour process the resulting liquid is exceptionally smooth with juniper and citrus notes and traces of rose hip and grapefruit.

Bombay Sapphire

Bombay Sapphire is the gin that gently led the category out of its dog days. Developed in the 1980s by Michel Roux, the driving force behind Absolut Vodka, it's a juniper-light premium gin that has attracted a whole new audience for gin. To the traditional botanicals are added a spicier coriander, orris root, liquorice, cassia bark, almonds, cubeb berries, and West African grains of paradise. It is made in a carterhead still through infusion to pick up these more subtle spicy and fragrant aromas. Stylish packaging and a distinctive blue bottle make Bombay Sapphire instantly recognisable on every back bar and its success has encouraged other gin distillers to experiment with innovative ingredients. Perhaps the biggest favour Bombay Sapphire has done for gin, however, is that it was the first brand to actually talk about what's inside the bottle. That got bartenders exploring different botanical flavours and Dick Bradsell's famous Bramble is believed to have been inspired by Bombay Sapphire. It's slightly sweet on the nose with delicate juniper, spice and lemon flavours.

Booth's Gin

Booth's is probably the oldest gin brand still in existence and dates back to around the 1740s, although there are records of the Booth family being involved in the wine trade as long ago as 1569. Philip Booth & Company Distillers in Clerkenwell are listed in a 1778 Directory of Merchants in London.

In 1819 Philip's son, Felix Booth, gained control of the business and built another distillery in Brentford on a quay by the Thames. Felix rapidly transformed Booth's into the largest distiller in the country. He was a philanthropist and was recognised for his public spiritedness in sponsoring John Ross's famous expedition to find the Northwest Passage. To this day large parts of Canada, Boothia Peninsula, Felix Harbour, Cape Felix and the Gulf of Boothia are rather oddly named after him. He also, at great personal cost, successfully lobbied for legislation to allow gin to be bottled in bond for export thus opening up the international gin export trade.

Booth's was family owned until 1896 when it became a limited company. In the 1930s, Booth's was one of the two top-selling gin brands in the world and the one most often specified in cocktail recipes. It remained hugely popular until the 1950s. The company made two London Dry style gins—Booth's Finest and Booth's High & Dry—as well as an Old Tom Gin. Booth's Finest is distinguished by its slight straw colour the result of ageing in oak barrel. They are no longer made in the UK but still available in the US where they have a loyal following. Diageo owns the Booth's brands.

Boudier Saffrom Gin

In the eighteenth and nineteenth centuries, there was a substantial gin industry in northern France which, let's not forget, was once part of the Low Countries and hence genever heartland. Saffron Gin, made by famous micro-distillers, Gabriel Boudier of Dijon, is a reminder of this history. Based on a nineteenth-century colonial recipe, Saffron Gin is rich in exotic botanicals which were the fashion at that time—juniper, coriander, lemon, orange peel, angelica seeds, iris, fennel and of course, saffron. Deep orange in colour, it's heavily infused with saffron and has a subtle spiciness derived from fennel and angelica seed. The ideal drinking occasion is as an apéritif served with tonic and a slice of orange to enhance the colour and flavour where it adds a whole new dimension of Campari-like herbal bitterness.

Broker's Gin

Brothers Martin and Andy Dawson created Broker's Gin in the late 1990s. It's a very English brand with its bowler hat and typical old-fashioned city gent pinstripe livery.

Broker's is batch-distilled in a copper pot-still made by John Dore, the Rolls Royce of still-makers, at the Langley Distillery. The botanical mix of juniper berries, coriander seeds, cassia bark, cinnamon, liquorice, orris, nutmeg, orange peel, lemon peel, angelica root is first steeped for 24 hours in triple-distilled neutral grain spirit made from 100% English wheat. It's a classic London Dry Gin with a rich aromatic nose and an intense flavour and makes no bones about it. The recipe is 200 years old, so all the botanicals are traditional, conventional gin botanicals: no off the wall ingredients. And its owners created it for people who really like gin and appreciate a big juniper hit. Spirits guru F Paul Pacult sums up the taste experience: "In the mouth it sits well on the tongue and, thankfully, is the proper level of alcohol for gin, 94 proof. It finishes long, semi-sweet, tangy and luscious. A superbly made London Dry Gin that deserves a very close look by any admirer of that style."

Bulldog

Although Bulldog Gin is owned by a former investment banker based in New York, it's a very classic London Dry Gin distilled in London and made from 100% British grain. Quadruple distilled and triple filtered for extra smoothness, Bulldog is made with unusually exotic botanicals that include lotus leaves, lavender, poppy and the reputedly aphrodisiac Dragon Eye, a cousin of the lychee fruit. It also has a distinctive look with a very butch smoked-grey tinted bottle and spiked collar. Big, bold flavours and a refreshingly crisp character make this one for a Martini especially the Dirty version.

Burnett's White Satin

Burnett's White Satin is a venerable English brand that was established by Robert Burnett in the late eighteenth century. He acquired a huge distillery in Vauxhall that had been built by in 1767 by Sir Joseph Mawbey. It was then the biggest distillery in London and ccontemporary reports record that there were seldom less than 2000 hogs constantly grunting, and kept entirely on the grains. (A common practice of distillers at the time was to keep pigs and feed them on the waste from distilling—very eco). Robert Burnett became Sheriff of London, in 1794, and was knighted the following year.

Burnett's White Satin is another classic brand that has experienced a rollercoaster ride. For years, it was one of the biggest selling gins in the UK but was then demoted to a cheap compounded gin made with a molasses spirit and artificial flavourings. Recently, however, it has returned to its roots as a traditionally distilled proper London Dry Gin made with grain spirit and natural botanicals. Crisp and clean on the nose it has warm spicy flavours, and a fresh, juniper palate.

Cadenhead's Old Raj

adenhead's Old Raj gin is actually neither a London or a Distilled gin and is technically made by cold compounding. The reason it's included here is because, despite that, it's a damn fine gin, probably because of its exceptionally high strength. Old Raj is made by steeping the botanicals in a mixture of alcohol and water, then distilling them separately in a small pot still. The resulting essence is then combined with a neutral grain spirit and saffron is added for colouring. At 46% ABV, it is spirity and peppery with a slight medicinal taste from the high alcohol content. At 55% it is very aromatic, full and rounded.

Caorunn Gin

nspired by Celtic tradition, Caorunn (pronounced "ka-roon") Gin is small batch gin made in Scotland by Inver House Distillers, the malt whisky experts. Made from a pure grain spirit and reduced with Scottish Highland water, it is distilled at the Balmenach Distillery. Caorunn is the Gaelic name for the rowan berry and the gin includes rowan berries and a further ten botanicals including six traditional ones plus some unusual, particularly Scottish ingredients such as Coul Blush apple, heather, bog myrtle and dandelion. The botanical infusion process is by virtue of a unique Copper Berry Chamber. Juniper balanced by the softness of heather honey and the sharp fruitiness of rowan makes Caorunn a big flavoursome gin that works well in the classic drinks and in punches.

Cascade Mountain Gin

Cascade Mountain Gin is made in the wilds of Oregon at the small Ben Distillery. Its major point of difference is that it uses locally-grown, wild juniper berries that are hand picked alongside other northwestern botanicals. The natural juniper gives this gin a very slight straw colour, which is not filtered out. Juniper dominates and at 95 proof Cascade Mountain Gin is not to be messed with.

Citadelle Gin

Made in Ars, France, by Cognac's Gabriel & An-
dreu according to a 1771 recipe that was created
by the Citadelle Distillery in Dunkirk—the old
genever heartland. Citadelle Gin has 19 botanicals including such rarities as savory, fennel, violets and star anise.
The use of so many botanicals somewhat stifles the juniper
but does give this gin unusual aromatic, herbal notes and
a pleasantly perfumed palate. A new Citadelle Réserve has
been launched in a limited edition. Aged for six months in
oak, it has a fuller juniper taste with a slight oakiness. Both
are bottled at 44% ABV or 88 proof.

Cork Dry Gin

Cork Dry Gin was first made at the Old Watercourse
Distillery—established near Cork in 1793—according to an original recipe, using spices and herbs
brought to the port of Cork. Now it's made at the Mid-
dleton Distilleries by Irish Distillers and bottled at 38%
ABV, which is not nearly as good as the export version at
43% ABV. Cork Dry is triple distilled and is sweeter than
many UK-produced dry gins as a result of the use of sweeter
citrus, reputedly tangerine. It is not a big juniper gin, but

has sherberty, mellow flavours that make it a good everyday gin. It's Ireland's biggest seller.

DH Krahn Gin

This relatively new US gin sits firmly in the London style tastewise, but is not produced like traditional London gins. It is made by macerating botanicals and then re-distilling them with neutral spirit in a patent Stupfler pot still. The gin is then left to age slightly in steel barrels so no colour is picked up. The recipe is simple with only six botanicals: Italian juniper, Moroccan coriander seed, Floridian oranges, Californian lemon and grapefruit and a touch of Thai ginger. The Thai ginger is an inspired ingredient adding an almost chilli tang to the sweet fruit and citrus profile. Ideal in a Martini.

Gilbey's Special Dry Gin

Established by brothers Walter and Alfred Gilbey, in 1857, on their return from service in the Crimean War, the Gilbey's empire eventually expanded to include a substantial wine and whisky business plus a large number of off-licence shops. But it was gin that made the Gilbey's name. In 1872, the brothers began to produce their own gin at their Camden Town Distillery. Earlier they had purchased the landmark Pantheon building in Oxford Street as offices.

Gilbey's Gin soon became the leading brand in British colonies. By the 1920s, distilleries had been built in Australia and Canada. During Prohibition, regular consignments of Gilbey's Gin were shipped to Antwerp and Hamburg. From there they travelled to just outside the 12-mile limit of the US coastline and were then smuggled into the States. In fact, so in demand was Gilbey's during Prohibition that it was widely counterfeited. The company introduced a special frosted bottle that was difficult to copy.

Now owned by Diageo, Gilbey's is no longer made in the UK and rarely seen there. It's produced in Australia, Canada, New Zealand, South Africa and the USA and remains a huge brand in the US and Commonwealth countries.

Gordon's Special Dry Gin

Alexander Gordon was born in London on 10 August 1742. His father, George Gordon, was a native of Aberdeen, who allegedly left Scotland due to his involvement in the 1715 Jacobite uprising. Alexander founded his distilling business in Southwark, in 1769, and then moved it, in 1786, to Clerkenwell. He had ten children, one of whom, Charles, carried on the family business when

Alexander died as an honoured citizen of London. His son, another Charles, sold the firm, in 1878, to John Currie & Co. Distillers at the Four Mills Distillery at Bromley by Bow, Currie & Co had provided Gordon's with spirit for rectification for many years. Tanqueray already had a close commercial relationship with Curries and, in 1898, Gordon and Tanqueray combined to create Tanqueray, Gordon & Co. This move established the two companies as the most powerful force in English distilling, a position they still hold.

Gordon's today is the number two selling global gin (only outsold by the vile Ginebra San Miguel made in the Philippines) with distilleries in the UK, the United States, Canada, South America and Jamaica.

Gordon's is a very traditional London gin made to the original recipe which specifies ginger, cassia oil and nutmeg as well as the more commonly found juniper and coriander. Sold in the UK at 37.5% ABV it is very juniper and lemony with a clean sharp aftertaste and works well in a Gin & Tonic, which is how it's mostly drunk. But Gordon's Export Strength at 47.3% ABV is a whole different ball game—more flavourful and more aromatic. A very interesting version— Gordon's Distiller's Cut—made with ginger and lemongrass was launched a few years ago. It was rashly discontinued which is a great pity. But it's still out there and worth tracking down if you can find it.

Greenall's Original London Dry

G & J Greenall has been producing gin since 1761, the year that Thomas Dakin built a distillery in the centre of Warrington, then a great centre for brewing and distilling. In 1870, Edward Greenall, a member of an established Lancashire brewing family, bought the Dakin company and acquired ownership of a successful business with an established distribution network.

In the mid-1960s, a new distillery, bottling facilities and warehouses were built on land close to the site of the original distillery. This allowed Greenall to expand into contract distilling. Disaster struck, in 2005, when the entire premises was almost destroyed by fire. But the distillery was saved and was able to continue to make a number of prestigious gins including Bombay Sapphire.

Greenall's own brands are excellent. Greenall's Original Gin contains eight different botanicals, including the less common cassia bark and ground almonds. It is distilled four times and made according to a 1761 recipe in a still that was built in 1831. It is bottled at 40% ABV (80 proof) and is strongly citrus on the nose, developing into dry rounded juniper notes. G & J Greenall Bloom is a recent arrival to the portfolio. It's a much more delicate, summery gin made with botanicals such as chamomile, pomelo, lavender and honeysuckle with a light, floral taste and strong violet notes. The company also makes a range of canned gin drinks and has huge markets in Eastern Europe, particularly in Russia, where people are regularly spotted downing them on the way to work in the morning.

G'Vine

G'Vine gins are the brainchild of EuroWineGate, the French company who make Ciroc, the first vodka made from grapes. The gins are produced from Ugni Blanc grapes that are distilled four times to create a grape neutral spirit. The base of G'Vine Floraison is unique as it consists of the rare vine flower, which blooms for a few days in June (this blossoming period is known in France as the *floraison*, hence the name). The flowers are immediately macerated in the grape neutral spirit for two to five days and then distilled in a small copper Florentine. Meanwhile nine botanicals—ginger root, liquorice, green cardamom, cassia bark, coriander, juniper berries, cubeb berries, nutmeg and lime—are infused in families (juniper berries, then spices, and then aromatics) in the grape neutral spirit for several days before distillation in small copper stills. Finally, the vine flower infusion, the three botanical distillates and more grape spirit are blended and copper-pot distilled one final time.

A new version, G'Vine Nouaison, named for the berry on the vine that grows into a grape, has increased juniper and nutmeg components, less vine flower and is bottled at a higher 43.9 % ABV. Whilst G'Vine gins may not be for the juniper enthusiast, their light, floaty, floral flavours come to the fore in citrus-based drink especially when lime is in the mix.

Hayman's Gins

Christopher Hayman inherited his passion for gin distilling from his great grandfather James Burrough who created Beefeater Gin in the 1800s. The Haymans are the oldest English distilling family still involved in the trade. Rather like their illustrious ancestor, Hayman's Distillers make several different types of gin. Hayman's London Dry Gin is a fine example of the classic hand-crafted London style. The mix of ten botanicals is steeped with triple-distilled neutral grain spirit in a traditional pot still for 24 hours before distilling begins. The result is a crisp and

elegant gin in which juniper, coriander and strong citrus elements are carefully balanced.

The company has also led the revival of Old Tom Gin. Hayman's Old Tom is distilled from an original family recipe from the 1870s. It's distilled in the traditional way with more pungent botanicals like nutmeg, cassia bark, cinnamon and liquorice layered on a juniper and citrus profile and sweetened with sugar. It's an authentic recreation of the Old Tom style once made by most English distillers with one crucial difference in that the spirit is properly rectified. It's much sought after by bartenders who want to experiment with original cocktail recipes from the glory days.

Hayman's 1820 Gin Liqueur is similar to the cordial gins of bygone days. It's made from 100% pure grain spirit and a subtle blend of botanicals with aromatic juniper and fruity notes. It's best served neat, on the rocks.

Hendrick's Gin

Some years ago, when whisky experts William Grant & Sons decided to apply their distilling expertise to the production of a new gin, the brief was to come up with a super premium that would be lighter and less juniper dominated than other gins on the market. The traditional tastes of English summer were to be the starting point. For months, the team worked in the lab, endlessly experimenting with different botanicals in the quest to get the right balance. It's not easy, as even minute quantities of a particular ingredient can alter the entire taste spectrum. After much trial and error, they arrived at the final botanicals—juniper, orris root, angelica, coriander, lemon and orange peel, caraway seeds, chamomile flowers, elderflowers, cubeb berries and meadowsweet with a final infusion of distilled oils of cucumber and Bulgarian *rosa damascena* [Damascus rose].

Having developed an unusual recipe, it's not surprising that William Grant should adopt a different approach to making their new baby. Hendrick's is small-batch distilled using two different methods—pot still and infusion. In the former, a quantity of botanicals and neutral grain spirit are placed in the distillery's Bennett pot still, dating from the

1860s, where it is gently "boiled" in the traditional way. A specially-adapted Carterhead still, one of only four in the world, is used for the infusion method (*see page 26*). Think of the different results you get when you steam vegetables. That is the effect—cleaner, more subtle flavours. The two distillates are then combined and cucumber and rose distillates added.

The percentages of pot distilled to infusion distilled is part of the secret recipe. But the combination of the strong, aromatic flavours achieved in a pot still with the more subtle, volatile flavours picked up in the Carterhead is obvious in the final taste of Hendrick's. It results in fresh, floral, slightly aromatic notes, combined with silky smooth texture and mouthfeel. Hendrick's is one of the gins that has led the renewed interest in gin and works particularly well in drinks like the Elderflower Collins and the Elderflower Martini.

Jensen's Bermondsey Gins

Jensen's Bermondsey Gin is the brainchild of Christian Jensen, a Danish IT specialist who fell in love with old-style gins while working in Japan. After trying all of the modern gins, he started tasting samples of older, heavier and more flavoursome gins—popular in the 1940s and earlier, when gin cocktails were in their heyday—and then approached a specialist London distillery to create something similar. After a long process his ideal recipe emerged. Since he is based in Bermondsey, he named the result Jensen's London-Distilled Dry Bermondsey Gin.

Here, the emphasis is on old-style botanicals and clean, fresh juniper-led flavours that are derived from a small number of classic ingredients such as juniper, coriander, orris root, angelica and liquorice. Bottled at 43% ABV, Jensen's is a taste of what London Dry used to be and rumour has it that it's a recreation of a once very famous brand—Nicholson's Lamplighter Gin. Its heavier, more aromatic style makes it a good choice for many of the classic gin drinks from the Golden Age of cocktails.

Jensen's London-Distilled Old Tom Gin is now also available. Its sweeter style is achieved by adding greater quantities of sweet botanicals, not sugar.

Junipero

Made by Anchor Distilling, the guys that kicked off the craft beer movement, Junipero Gin is produced at a craft distillery situated on Portrero Hill in San Francisco. It is a classic Dry style of gin made with 12 botanicals in a small copper pot still. Its makers are coy about the exact ingredients, but tasting reveals strong juniper, liquorice and grapefruit as well as other citrus. At 49.3% ABV, it's a big complex gin with a pronounced spiciness.

Larios Gin

Spain is the second largest gin market in the world. There are numerous Spanish-made gin brands, some very local. The only international brand is Larios, which dominates the domestic market and, indeed, is the fourth biggest gin worldwide. Larios Gin is very much in the London Dry style in that is it is double distilled, aromatic and unsweetened with strong juniper flavours evident. For years, there was a question mark over the kind of spirit that Larios was based on. But nowadays the quality is consistently good.

Bottled at 40% ABV, it is drunk in vast quantities either in a Gin & Tonic or the famous Gin Larios con Coca Cola, which, surprisingly enough, is not half bad. The company recently launched a premium expression, Larios 12, named after its twelve botanicals: juniper, coriander, nutmeg, angelica and masses of citrus in the form of lemon, orange, mandarin, tangerine, clementine, watermelon and lime. Here, the spirit and the botanicals are distilled four times and a fifth distillation adds an infusion of orange blossom.

London Hill Gin

The epitome of the London Dry style, London Hill Gin is made by whisky experts Ian Macleod Distillers in Scotland. It's made in the traditional way in copper pot stills and, in addition to the four core botanicals, London Hill also uses cassia, ginger, nutmeg and liquorice, which give a very rounded profile with juniper just edging it in terms of taste. London Hill gin consistently wins awards at spirit competitions. Yet it's a gin with a very low profile and is not nearly as widely recognised as it deserves to be.

Magellan Gin

French gin, Magellan, is named after the famous sixteenth -century Portuguese explorer Ferdinand Magellan, who led an epic around the world voyage. Although he was killed in the Philippines, his ship returned laden with cloves. A signature botanical of this rather stylish presented gin, cloves are accompanied by cinnamon, cassia, nutmeg and grains of paradise alongside the conventional gin botanicals. Made from triple-distilled French wheat that is re-distilled with the botanicals, a final infusion of iris results in a deep blue colour.

Martin Miller's Gin

The creation of Martin Miller, publisher of the famous Miller's Antique Price Guides, Martin Miller's Gin is made at the Langley Distillery in the Black Country, using traditional methods and craftsmanship. A century-old gem of a copper pot still named "Angela" is the star of the show. Before distillation, the grain spirit and the botanicals are left to steep overnight in her generous expanse. The botanicals recipe is a taste feast with juniper and other common botanicals like coriander, angelica, orange peel and orris root, but also the less often used cassia and cinnamon bark, ground nutmeg and liquorice plus one other secret ingredient, believed to be cucumber. Like all gins, Martin Miller's is reduced with water to its bottling strength of 40% ABV. Miller's Gin however takes this to an almost obsessive extreme transporting the elixir on a 3,000-mile round trip to Borganes in Iceland to be blended with what is considered to be the purest water on the planet. Filtered through lava formed millions of years ago, Icelandic glacial water imparts a freshness and smoothness to the taste of Martin Miller's, whilst also contributing greatly to its much-vaunted texture. The end result of all this hard work is a gin that is gentle in the mouth with fragrant, slightly spicy aromas and strong hints of Parma violet and lavender. This unique taste profile makes Martin Miller's the ideal gin for a host of new wave gin drinks with fresh, clean, natural flavours.

Martin Miller's Westbourne Strength

Named after Martin Miller's original base in Westbourne Grove, West London, Martin Miller's Westbourne Strength Gin is made in exactly the same way as Martin Miller's Gin. Same botanicals, same spirit, same pot still methods. The major difference is that it is bottled at the much higher 45.2% ABV. At this

strength, the taste profile veers towards the more classic London flavour with lots of delicious juniper, spice and citrus flavours. The quality of Martin Miller's Westbourne Strength Gin has been recognised by numerous awards in prestigious spirit competitions around the world.

No. 3 St. James

No. 3 St James London Dry Gin is produced by iconic spirits company Berry Bros & Rudd and named for the address of the premises founded in 1698 by the Widow Bourne in the heart of London. That original shop is still the oldest wine and spirit merchant in the UK and a Mecca for lovers of fine drink. Made in Schiedam, Holland's distilling centre and gin's ancestral home, No 3 St. James is a classic London Dry Gin bottled at a serious 46% ABV. The botanical mix of juniper, coriander, sweet orange peel, angelica, grapefruit peel and cardamom is left to steep overnight before distillation in traditional copper pot stills. On the nose there's and instant and welcome hit of piney juniper with citrus and coriander very evident. In the mouth the juniper develops into a crispness nicely balanced by a soft spiciness. A classic.

No. 209 Gin

No. 209 Gin is made at Distillery 209 on Pier 50 in San Francisco, which is also allegedly the birthplace of the Gin Martini. The original 209 Gin Distillery was located on a Napa Valley wine estate that was purchased, in 1999, by food entrepreneur Leslie Rudd. He restored the actual building to its former glory. But its size and location were not suitable for his dream of reviving the distillery, so new premises were purchased in the city and No. 209 was reborn.

No. 209 Gin is made in a specially-commissioned Scottish copper pot still based on the design of the Glenmorangie whisky stills, which were in fact originally used for making gin. It's a robust gin that is built around the signature botanicals of bergamot, sweet orange, cardamom and cassia as well as the more usual juniper and citrus. They are macerated in the still overnight and each distillation takes around 11 hours. Unlike most gins, No. 209 is not made from concentrated gin that is then reduced with water (AKA: the two-shot method). Rather, each "single-shot" distillation comes off the still ready to be bottled. On the palate, there are very pleasant lavender and floral notes that combine well with the bittersweet juniper. A four-times column-distilled spirit made from Midwestern corn imparts a smooth, slightly sweet finish. Bartenders recommend No. 209 in a Gin Mojito.

Oxley Classic English Gin

This new ultra premium from the Bacardi-owned Oxley Spirits Company was eight years in development and has certainly brought something new and exciting to the gin scene. In a major technological advance

it is the first ever spirit created by the cold distillation method. So instead of heat being applied to redistil the spirit with the botanicals, vacuum is used to reduce the pressure in the still and lower the temperature to approximately -5° C. At this temperature the spirit, which has been macerated for 15 hours, becomes vapour. It then meets a cold finger probe (chilled to -100° C) and reverts back to spirit to be collected for bottling.

The bespoke still at London's Thames Distillers produces only 120 bottles per batch and a major advantage of cold distillation is that there are no heads or tails—so less wastage than traditional distillation methods. The most obvious benefit however is the taste of the final product, which is exceptionally clean and fresh. Oxley's 14 botanicals include the traditional flavourings as well as three different types of fresh citrus—grapefruit, orange and lemon—and exotics like vanilla and meadowsweet. Slightly spicy on the nose with hints of lavender, almond, marshmallow and soft citrus, juniper is evident but not dominant. Think soft and scented rather than oily and pungent. The thing that stands out however is the texture and purity of the spirit that is holding these complex aromas together. At 47% ABV Oxley is a big gin but it's very smooth and lush, almost creamy. Recommended serve is straight over ice in a balloon glass with a grapefruit twist.

Plymouth Gin

In the eighteenth century Plymouth, London, Bristol, Warrington and Norwich were the great gin distilling centres, each producing their own unique style of gin. Gradually the London Dry style came to dominate. But the gin made in Plymouth retained its own distinctively aromatic character. Plymouth Gin has remained true to this tradition. Produced in a still which has not been changed for over 150 years, it has a subtle, full bodied flavour with no bitter botanicals and not nearly as much of a juniper hit as some gins. A higher than usual proportion of root ingredi-

ents is the source of Plymouth's distinctive, earthy, rooty tastes, whilst the addition of sweet orange and cardamom impart a softly fruity, spicy finish. Pure water from Dartmoor contributes to Plymouth Gin's exceptionally clean and fresh flavour.

Plymouth Gin has a long history and dates back to at least 1793. But the Black Friars building in Plymouth, in which it is made, goes back to the 1400s and there is reason to believe that distilling may have been carried out on these premises as long ago as the sixteenth century. Certainly Black Friars can rightly claim to be the oldest working in distillery in the UK. It is also reputed to have been the place where the Pilgrim fathers gathered before they set off in the *Mayflower*, in 1620, for America.

Plymouth Gin is the only UK gin to have a geographic designation like an *appellation controllée*: the result of a legal judgement in the 1880s when a London distiller began producing a Plymouth gin. Coates & Co won the suit, establishing that Plymouth Gin could only be made in Plymouth, by law.

One of the world's great gin brands, Plymouth Gin suffered years of neglect in the hands of the multinationals who never really appreciated its heroic qualities and heritage. But it's now firmly ensconced as a sister brand to Beefeater and Beefeater 24. Plymouth Original is produced at 41.2% ABV (83 degrees proof), whilst Plymouth Navy Strength is bottled at a whopping 57% ABV. Plymouth also produces Sloe Gin, Damson Gin and a Fruit Cup.

Right Gin

The makers of Right Gin deliberately set out to explore gin outside the London style box and have come up with a powerful, unconventional gin. It's made in Sweden from North American corn that is distilled five times, but retains a lingering faint sweetness. The botanicals recipe has juniper, coriander leaf (not the more common seed), cardamom, lemon peel, bergamot, bitter orange and Sarawak pepper from Borneo. Each botanical ingredient is

distilled separately and then combined with the spirit. Pure Swedish water is then used to reduce the gin to 40% ABV. Right Gin delivers bold flavours with warm, nutty aromas and lingering pepper notes and tastes great in the classic cocktails.

Rogue Spruce Gin

Artisanally distilled in Oregon, Rogue Spruce Gin has won numerous awards in prestigious spirits competitions. Made from twelve botanicals that consist of the traditional ones plus spruce oil, whole cucumbers, ginger, grains of paradise and tangerine. Spruce is a coniferous tree closely related to juniper. So one might think: that's far too much pine going on. But where juniper has a fragrant lavender taste, spruce has a sharper fruitier tang and the combination works. Spruce Gin has a heavy texture with quite a lot of oiliness but clean, tangy evergreen aromas come through nicely. Works particularly well in cocktails like the Bramble or other drinks with dark berries. And it is a great partner for drinks made with sloe gin. There's also a Spruce Pink version, which is aged in Oregon pinot noir barrels making it slightly fruitier and definitely pink.

Seagram's Gins

Seagram's Extra Dry is the US equivalent of Gordon's in the UK—a huge volume brand that outsells its nearest competitors by far. For that reason, it is not appreciated as much as it really ought to be. Known as "the smooth gin in the bumpy bottle", it's made in the USA from 100% American grain neutral spirit that is distilled with juniper, coriander, orris, angelica, cardamom, and cassia bark. It is then mellowed in charred white oak barrels, which gives it a slightly golden hue. It has candied fruit, citrus and juniper on the nose, then a slightly sweet sherbet palate with spice and floral hints and is bottled at 40% ABV.

Seagram's Distiller's Reserve is the combination of the best of the barrels as selected out of hundreds by Seagram's Master Distiller. The higher strength of the spirit at 51% ABV is definitely noticeable when sipped straight.

Sipsmith London Dry Gin

Sipsmith London Dry Gin is produced in the first new distillery licensed in London in nearly two hundred years. It is made in the former office of the late renowned whisky and beer writer Michael Jackson. The spirit is made by hand in genuinely small batches—never

more than 500 bottles a time, often considerably less—by Master Distiller Jared Brown and proprietors Stamford Galsworthy and Fairfax Hall. It is first and foremost, a classic London Dry Gin, tempered with a touch of the more floral Plymouth style. The aroma is of citrus and field flower blossoms, balanced with sweet citrus peel, and herbaceous notes reminiscent of a meadow on a warm summer day. On the palate it reveals high quality spirit, distinctive juniper, sweet orange and lemon marmalade, leading to a long, slightly savory finish with a hint of black pepper. This makes it an ideal spirit for a Gin & Tonic or Gin Collins.

Tanqueray Gins

Charles Tanqueray, born in 1810, was the descendant of Huguenots and came from a long line of clergymen. Between 1828 and 1830, he set out to establish himself as a distiller— a choice of profession that would once have been criticised, but distilling was by now something with which a gentleman could be associated. The business of Edward & Charles Tanqueray & Co, Rectifiers was established, by 1838, on Vine Street at the southern edge of

Bloomsbury in the parishes of St George, Bloomsbury and St Giles in the Fields. It was known, by 1847, as Charles Tanqueray & Co. However, according to a property deed of the same year, the site had been used as a distillery for some time. A price list of 1895 from W A Taylor & Co of New York illustrates a bottle of Tanqueray's Finest Old Tom, with the caption, "The Bloomsbury Distillery, established 1757".

In his Bloomsbury Distillery, Charles Tanqueray wanted to produce a quality gin. He started with the pure waters of Finsbury spa, a district of rolling countryside and crystal clear streams, then just outside London. After years of experimenting with ingredients, Charles Tanqueray finally produced his unique recipe.

Tanqueray Gin met with instant success and, remaining records show, a small but prestigious clientele. Soon, Tanqueray stoneware crocks, used in the trade until 1900 were to be seen in the better class of grocer and wine and spirit merchants as well as in discerning households. (He did not deal in bulk-casked gin for ordinary taverns.) Within a few years, Tanqueray Gin was being exported to the British Colonies while still much in demand at home.

Today, the Tanqueray name is found on three quite different gins. Tanqueray Special Dry Gin is a London Dry with knobs on, greeting one boisterously with a lovely juniper fresh welcome. Although the original Tanqueray recipe is still secret, Special Dry is believed to contain only four botanicals, proof that sometimes more is less and that the balance of ingredients is key to its taste. On tasting, juniper and liquorice are very obvious as is a subtle spiciness most likely derived from coriander. At a high-strength 47% ABV, based on a clean grain spirit, it is exceptionally dry and somehow very sophisticated. There's also a 43.1% ABV version, which is just as good.

Launched in 2000, Tanqueray 10 is a new luxury Tanqueray gin bottled at 47.3% ABV. Made in small batches, it adds fresh citrus in the form of limes, oranges and white grapefruit to the botanical mix. The citrus is distilled with pure grain spirit in a swan neck still known as "Tiny Ten". The resulting spirit is then distilled with the more traditional botanicals such as juniper, coriander, angelica and liquorice. Extra fresh citrus is added to the final spirit. Juniper is at the heart of this gin ,but is relatively laid back when compared to big gins like Beefeater and Tanqueray Special Dry. It's very citrusy, clean and as fresh as a meadow with soothing notes of chamomile. Tanqueray 10 was created specifically for Martinis and owner Diageo has set up the Tanqueray 10 Guild with ten top bartenders from ten cities around the world, who have developed their own signature Martinis. So, for example, Colin Field of the Hemingway Bar at the Ritz

Paris freezes both the glass and the Tanqueray 10 to -18.3°C precisely, and adds three olives but no vermouth.

Tanqueray Rangpur is the latest addition to the Tanqueray family. Made with fresh Rangpur limes, juniper and bay leaf, it is midway between a traditional Dry and a fruit gin with a distinctive lime taste. Mix with cranberry juice for a Rangpur Cran or with ginger ale and a few drops of bitters for a Rangpur Ginger.

The London Gin

The London Gin—one of a handful of new wave gins actually distilled in London—is blue: the colour is derived from gardenia. Its base is a spirit made from Suffolk and Norfolk grain. In line with the classic gins of yesteryear, juniper, coriander and angelica feature in the recipe of thirteen botanicals which also includes orris root, orange and lemon peel, liquorice root, savory, cinnamon and cassia bark. The London Gin throws bergamot into the mix—that instantly recognisable perfumed aroma in Earl Grey tea. Its citric qualities marry well with the fresh juicy flavours of orange and lemon peel, whilst the bergamot also reinforces the "holding" role of orris root. Rested for three weeks after distillation in a pot still, the result is a very English style Distilled Gin. At a generous 47% ABV,

The London Gin is delicate and elegant on the nose with marked spicy and balsamic notes. Soft, elegant and mellow in the mouth, it's a sophisticated, well-rounded gin that delivers in every area.

Voyager Gin

Another US artisan boutique gin from a small family-owned distillery in the Pacific Northwest, Voyager starts life as a Kentucky neutral grain spirit. The botanical recipe of juniper, coriander, licorice, cardamom, anise, lemon, orange, orris, angelica, and cassia is distilled together with the spirit in a small copper pot still. It is produced in single batches: Each batch makes about thirty 12-bottle cases. Only the heart of the distillation is taken. One point of difference here is that the botanicals are all organic, imported from the best organic growers from around the world. The still-strength spirit is brought down to bottling proof of by adding purified Cascade Mountain water.

Whitley Neill London Dry

Whitley Neill is a relatively new premium London Dry Gin, independently owned and created by Johnny Neill, the fourth generation of the Greenall Whitley distilling family.

Whitley Neill is a handcrafted gin made from a 100% grain spirit that is steeped with the botanicals prior to distillation in antique copper pot stills. The recipe took some time to formulate as the producers were determined to bring something new to the party. The result is nine botanicals consisting of core botanicals and the addition of two signature elements from Africa—the Cape Gooseberry and the fruit of the Baobob tree, the tree of life. The taste experience starts with a spicy freshness on the nose. Laid-back juniper and citrus combine with the fresh tanginess quality of the wild fruit to create robust yet delicate and clean flavours. A pleasant lingering finish holds those flavours in the mouth whilst an alcoholic strength of 42% ABV ensures perfect balance.

Xorigeur Gin, Gin de Mahon

X origuer Gin De Mahon is the only other gin with a geographic destination: it can only be made in Mahon on the Balearic island of Menorca. Gin distilling there dates from the British presence in the eighteenth century when Menorca was an important British base. British soldiers and sailors stationed in Mahon wanted gin, the fashionable spirit at home. Enterprising local distilleries started making it from juniper berries, distilled with a spirit made from the local wine.

The Xoriguer distillery, founded and still owned by the Pons family, is now the only gin distillery on the island. There, Gin de Mahon is made as it always has been from a wine distillate in ancient copper stills heated by wood burning fires. When it comes off the still it is stored in large oak barrels and bottled at 40% ABV.

Only members of the Pons family know the secrets of the recipe for Xoriguer. It certainly has juniper and other aromatic herbs. Tasting reveals a brandy-like flavour with notes of caraway, fennel and orris. Xoriguer Gin is sold in green glass bottles with handles that copy the old Dutch stone crocks. It is drunk widely on the island particularly during the summer-long season of fiestas when it is mixed with lemonade in a drink called Pomada. It tastes innocuous but be warned, it packs a real punch.

Zephyr Gin

Named after the Greek god of the west wind, Zephyr is a small-batch distilled gin produced by re-distilling neutral grain spirit with natural botanicals such as juniper berries, citrus peel, and coriander seeds. There are two versions. Black Zephyr uses elderflower and sweet elderberry alongside the more conventional botanicals. Blu Zephyr [yes, it's Blu Zephyr] adds a final infusion of sweet elderberry and gardenia for smoothness and colour. The 40% ABV of these gins and their very fruity floral notes create endless possibilities for experimentation in classic and modern cocktails.

Zuidam Gin

This high strength 44.5% ABV Dry gin from the family-owned Zuidam Distillers in Holland, is a real gin lover's gin. It contains nine botanicals: juniper berries and iris root from Italy, coriander from Morocco, angelica root, fresh sweet oranges and lemons from Spain, real whole bean vanilla from Madagascar, liquorice root from India, cardamom pods from Sri Lanka. Unlike most gins that add all the botanicals simultaneously, Zuidam distils each ingredient or botanical separately and then marries the nine different distillates together according to their secret recipe. Patrick van Zuidam believes that by distilling separately, he can extract the purest flavours from the botanicals. The result is a big gin, strong in juniper but with a fiery sweetness. Zuidam also makes an excellent Genever Gin based on

a malt spirit distilled together with juniper, liquorice root, vanilla, aniseed and marjoram. It's decidedly sweeter than the Dry with a malty undertone. Unlike some genevers, it's crystal clear.

FRUIT GINS

All of the old distillers made a vast range of fruit-flavoured gins. Orange and Lemon Gins lasted well into the twentieth century. But the fashion for fruit gins seems to have largely disappeared with one notable exception—Sloe Gin.

Sloe Gin is described as a "British liqueur". It's made by steeping wild sloe berries, the fruit of the blackthorn tree, in gin and allowing the flavours to marry. Both Gordon's and Plymouth make Sloe Gin. Another traditional brand, Hawker's Sloe Gin, has just come back into production. Once the favourite drink of prim Victorian ladies and the tweed clad, Sloe Gin has made the leap from the hip flasks of the hunting, fishing and shooting set to the backs of the most stylish bars. There's now a raft of new ways of drinking Sloe Gin in cocktails and long drinks that tie in with the fashion for drinking seasonally, using locally sourced ingredients. Try it with English apple juice, garnished with an apple slice. Or add 25 ml of Sloe Gin to champagne or sparkling wine for an apéritif that not only tastes great but also looks very pretty. Sloe Gin is also delicious on its own: an excellent alternative to brandy or port as an after-dinner drink.

Sloe Gin is easy to make. Gather your sloe berries. Old railway lines are a good source for some reason. Fill a gin bottle half way with sloes, add 2 inches of castor sugar and top up with full-strength gin. Leave for several weeks to mature. Shake the bottle every now and again, if you re-member, and there it is.

FRUIT CUPS

The famous Pimm's No 1 fruit cup was invented, in 1840, by James Pimm in London. He owned a chain of restaurants all over the City and made a gin drink blended with liqueurs, herbs and spices that he sold to his customers in pint tankards. In 1859, he started bottling it for sale in other bars and restaurants. The company was sold to Sir Horatio Davis, a city entrepreneur, who developed an export trade for Pimm's. One of the first-recorded exports was to the famous Galle Face Hotel in Colombo, Sri Lanka.

Pimm's was also sent up the Nile, in 1898, to the forces at Khartoum and Omdurman in the Sudan.

Other Pimm's cups were introduced, based on Scotch (No 2), brandy (No 3), rum (No 4), rye whisky (No 5) and vodka (No 6). But the gin-based Pimm's No 1 remains the taste of English summer. Plymouth Gin also makes an excellent gin-based Fruit Cup.

DUTCH GENEVER

If you're a fan of Dutch genever, a visit to Schiedam, just outside Rotterdam, is an absolute must. The town is as important to Dutch spirits as the Scottish Highlands is to whisky. In 1880, Schiedam boasted 392 distilleries and its economy was entirely based around genever, with hundreds of cooperages, brass and cork factories, malt houses, yeast makers and glass works. Twenty huge windmills, the largest in the world, ground grain to feed the stills. The Museum of Genever in Schiedam is crammed with information and also has a working distillery making traditional, maltwine genever.

Although Dutch genever is no longer the fashionable drink it once was, there are still over 200 brands on the market, including fruit-flavoured ones. Many are small local brands. Large producers like Bols and De Kuypers make the biggest brands. Bols is the oldest distilling firm in Holland and, at its vast premises in Zoetermeer, makes a number of different types of genever, including the recently launched Bols Genever in its stylish modern packaging. De Kuyper was founded in 1695 and still produces an excellent jonge graanjenever and an oude genever, but is now better known for their vast range of liqueurs.

There are also interesting craft genever brands like Zuidam and those made by AV Wees that are attracting attention from the bartending fraternity.

THE GREAT GIN DRINKS

Whilst there are many ways to drink gin this book will confine itself to the all time classics and some modern variations. There's a story behind most of them.

THE GIN & TONIC

Gin and tonic water is as quintessentially English as bacon and eggs or tea and cucumber sandwiches. With the sharp, piney flavour of juniper balancing the bitter sweetness of tonic, it's so perfect a match one would almost think they had been invented with each other in mind. But each half of this iconic partnership has its own quite distinctive story.

Like gin, tonic water began life as a medicine, its principal flavour derived from quinine bark, the well-known antidote to malaria. Reputedly, it all started in Peru, in 1638, when the wife of the Spanish Viceroy, Countess Chinchona, was cured of fever by a local medicine man using the bark of the native quina tree. In gratitude, she vowed to make her miraculous healing widely known. On her return to Spain, she took quantities of the bark back to the family estate at Chinchon, outside Madrid (where the town of Chinchon still exists). The fame of this magical substance that we know as quinine—but is botanically named *cinchona officinalis*, in honour of the Countess—spread throughout Europe. Used to cure both Charles II of England and the son of Louis XIV of France, the powdered bark became more precious than gold and just as hard to come by. In the mid-nineteenth century, the German explorer Dr Hasskari solved the supply problem by smuggling seeds of the cinchona tree from South America to Indonesia. From about 1867 onwards, cinchona was widely cultivated in Java, India, Ceylon and Jamaica.

Quinine was prescribed to both prevent and treat malaria and the bark was urgently needed throughout the tropics where malaria was rife. The British in India masked the bitter flavour of quinine with sugar and diluted the mixture with water to make it drinkable in the daily doses given to soldiers and other functionaries of the British Raj. It wasn't long before some bright spark realised that gin would enliven the medicine and the ideal sun-downer was born.

Returning expats brought the taste for this exotic drink home with them where it became known as "Indian Tonic Water". Commercial production of "Tonic Brewed Drinks" began in the nineteenth century. They were usually a combination of quinine salt that was rendered soluble in citric acid, which was blended with other bitter ingredients such as cassia or gentian, chiretta and horehound. One of the first to market was the "improved aerated tonic liquid" which was patented, in 1858, by Erasmus Bond.

For many years modern commercially produced tonic water contained no quinine at all. There are now several excellent authentic tonic waters available such as Fentimans, Fevertree and Q.

THE PERFECT GIN & TONIC

You wouldn't think it was necessary to give instructions for this very common drink but the G & T has been very badly let down by pub bartenders who serve it too weak, with not enough ice and flat tonic water from a gun. Made properly and drunk at the right time a Gin & Tonic is the perfect drink. Follow these simple rules:

- Always use a good quality gin.
- Use a single serve bottle or can of tonic water.
- Take a tall glass with a heavy bottom, which makes the bubbles in the tonic, last longer. Fill it with ice (at least four large cubes) and add a generous measure of gin. Pour in enough tonic to fill the glass. What you're aiming for is just over double the amount of tonic to gin.
- Add a freshly cut wedge of lemon or lime and rub it around the rim of the glass first. Some gin fans claim that lemon or lime spoils the flavour of the more citrus gins. Chacun a sa gout. Stir gently with a teaspoon or a cocktail stirrer.

THE DRY MARTINI

Only one thing can be said about the Dry Martini, The King of Cocktails, without provoking a storm of debate: It is American, and as the humorist HL Mencken described, it is "the only American invention as perfect as the sonnet." It was probably invented shortly after the end of the American Civil War since a drink called the Martinez was already featured in 1880s bartenders' manuals. By the 1890s, Martini was the more common name for the drink that by now was a mixture of sugar syrup, bitters, Old Tom Gin, red Italian vermouth and a squeeze of lemon peel.

With the increasing domination of Dry gin, the recipe became less sweet and drier and the formula became established as the one we know today: gin, French vermouth, an olive and/or a twist of lemon. Then the debate moved on to the exact proportions of the ingredients with some proposing a 7:1 gin to vermouth ratio whilst others advocated 4:1. Hardcore Martini fans like Spanish filmmaker Luis Bunuel "simply allowed a ray of sunlight to shine through a bottle of Noilly Prat before it hits the bottle of gin." Winston Churchill apparently just bowed in the direction of France as he measured his Plymouth Gin into a glass with an olive.

Nowadays, the fashion for Dry Martinis is very dry indeed. Even though minute quantities of vermouth are used, a Gin Martini made this way still tastes remarkably different from neat gin with an olive.

The recipe for two Gin Martinis is simple, yet precise:

> Into a cold metal shaker filled with ice pour
> 1 tablespoon dry vermouth to coat the ice.
> Strain off the excess vermouth and pour in
> 7 oz [210 ml] of gin. Stir until ice cold. Then
> strain into two cold cocktail glasses. Either zest
> the oil from 2 strips of lemon peel over each
> glass or garnish each drink with a single olive.
> A small, pickled cocktail onion makes it a
> Gibson.

Ask for a Dry Martini in a bar and the bartender will practically hug you as mixing a Martini is the ultimate test of cocktail skill. Everyone has his or her own theories. It's also a bit of a test of drinking skill and should be approached with caution. As the old joke goes "the Martini is like a woman's breasts because one is not enough and three's too many". Or as Dorothy Parker put it:

> "I like to have a Martini
> Two at the very most

After three I'm under the table

After four I'm under the host"

For many Martini fans however, the Dry Martini is the Little Black Dress of the cocktail world. You don't wear it every day. You don't even wear it at every party. But as soon as you've got it on, you know that it was the right choice.

THE NEGRONI

The Negroni is *la dolce vita* in a glass, summoning up images of all that is best about the Italian way of life. It's an exquisitely simple drink that real gin lovers love and it's one of the few classic cocktails whose provenance can be traced to a specific time and place. Imagine the scene: the Bar Casoni in Florence, circa 1920, where patrons are enjoying their Americanos, a drink made with Campari, sweet vermouth and soda water, named thus because of pro-American feelings after World War I. The Americano was the most fashionable drink of the day. But one regular had his own ideas about what made the perfect apéritif. Every day, Count Camillo Negroni ordered his Americano to be made with gin and without soda water.

Soon his friends began to request their drinks "the Negroni way." A classic was born.

The Negroni became the favourite drink of the Italian Futurists, the avant-garde literary and artistic movement led by Filippo Tommaso Marinetti. Today, along with many other gin cocktails from the Great Cocktail Age of the 1920s, it has become ultra fashionable again. The recipe goes like this:

> Equal parts of gin, Campari and red vermouth such as Cinzano or Martini Rosso. (Although bartenders like to play with more aromatic vermouths like Punt e Mes.)

> Combine all the ingredients in mixing glass filled with ice.Stir gently and pour into an old-fashioned glass.Add a hefty orange slice as a garnish.

PINK GIN

Traditionally the drink of officers and gentlemen, "Pinkers—as it is known—is a very British drink which is, once again, derived from the drinking habits of the Royal Navy, who were prescribed Angostura bitters as a cure for seasickness.

The recipe is simple: swirl several drops of Angostura bitters around in a tumbler-type glass. Shake out the residue and add 1.5 shots [37.5 ml] of gin. In the days of the Raj, the addition of tiny onions marinated in chilli turned a Pink Gin into a Gin Piaj. No ice. Remember: it's British.

THE GIMLET

This very simple combination of gin and Rose's Lime Juice dates back to 1867 when Lachlan Rose came up with a formula to preserve fruit juice without alcohol. It was invaluable as scurvy, caused by a deficiency of vitamin C, was still a major danger for sailors on long sea voyages. That same year a law required all vessels, Royal Navy and Merchant, to carry lime juice as a daily ration to their crews. This led to the remarkable success of Rose's Lime Juice and along the way resulted in British sailors being called "limeys". The Gimlet is named after a naval surgeon, Dr Gimlette, who spiced up his daily ration of Rose's with gin. It was also the favourite drink of Philip Marlowe, Raymond Chandler's ultra cool private detective hero.

This drink requires only two ingredients and simple execution:

> 1 part gin
> 1 part Rose's Lime Juice (it really doesn't work with fresh lime juice)

> Pour ingredients into a mixing glass three quarters filled with ice cubes. Stir until ice cold. Strain into a chilled martini glass. Garnish with a slice of lime peel.

THE WHITE LADY

This drink was invented during the Great Cocktail Age of the 1920s by legendary Scottish bartender, Harry MacElhone, who owned and operated Harry's New York Bar in Paris. He presided over the famous Ciro's Club in London before moving on, in 1923, to Paris. This delicious citrus-laden cocktail inspired and still inspires the creation of many others.

> 2 shots [50 ml] gin
> 3/4 [18.75 ml] shot Cointreau
> 3/4 shot [18.75 ml] freshly-squeezed lemon juice
> 1/4 shot [6.25 ml] sugar syrup

1/2 egg white

Shake with ice, strain into a chilled martini
glass and garnish with a lemon twist.

NEW WAVE GIN COCKTAILS

Alll of the great cocktails were originally invented
as gin drinks. Nouveau bartenders love playing
around with gin as different botanical profiles
give them scope for invention. New gins with floral and spicy
notes suit new-wave recipes like the ones outlined below:

The Bramble

(Invented by Dick Bradsell)

2 shots [50 ml] gin
1 shot [25 ml] fresh-squeezed lemon juice
½ [12.5 ml) shot simple syrup
½ [12.5 ml) shot crème de mure

Shake the first three ingredients over ice
and strain into an old-fashioned glass filled
with crushed ice. Slowly drizzle the crème de
mure through the crushed ice to create a "mar-
bled effect" and garnish with blackberries and
a lemon slice.

Lime and Coriander Martini

2 shots [50 ml] gin
1/2 shot [12.5 ml] freshly squeezed lime juice
1/2 shot [12.5ml] simple syrup
12- 15 leaves fresh coriander

Muddle the coriander leaves with lime juice and simple syrup. Add the gin and fill the shaker with ice. Shake, then double strain into a cocktail glass. Rim glass with a piece of sliced fresh chilli, then drop it into the glass.

Crimson Fizz

2 shots [50 ml] gin
1 tablespoon simple syrup
6 fresh strawberries
Soda water

Muddle the strawberries into a shaker. Add remaining ingredients and ice. Shake vigorously for several minutes, then strain into cold collins or fizz glass. Fizz up with bottled soda water, stirring continuously as the water is added. The point of this drink is that it should be served foamy and fizzy.

Elderflower Collins

(A new version of the classic Collins)

2 shots [50 ml] gin
2 shots [50 ml] lemon juice
½ [12.5 ml) shot elderflower cordial
½ [12.5 ml) shot simple syrup

Build all of the ingredients in the glass. Stir
well with a barspoon. Fizz up with bottled soda
water, stirring continuously as water is added.
Add ice.

Waterloo Sunset

**(A reworking of the classic champagne cock-
tail by Dan Warner)**

3/4 shot [approx 20 ml] gin
½ [12.5 ml] shot elderflower cordial
4 shots [100 ml] Perrier Jouët champagne
¼ [6 ml) shot créme de framboise

Stir gin and elderflower cordial in a bar glass or
shaker filled with ice. Strain into a flute glass.
Using the spiral of a bar spoon layer the champagne on top. Then layer the crème de framboise with a bar spoon. Garnish with a speared
raspberry.

Bittered Sling

35 ml gin
10 ml Mandarine Napoleon liqueur
25 ml elderflower cordial
25 ml freshly squeezed lemon juice
10 ml Benedictine

Soda water
Shake all ingredients, except the soda water,
over ice and strain into a sling glass filled with
cubed ice. Top up with soda water and garnish
with fresh apple slices.

INDEX

A

Act
  of 1736 49; of 1825 11; Tippling 59
almond 17, 30, 85, 87, 115
angelica 14, 15, 18, 25, 29, 30, 40, 66, 85, 87, 88, 91, 92, 105,
       107, 109, 110, 112, 119, 122, 123, 124, 127
aniseed 40, 128
aqua vitae 43, 45, 46

B

Belgium 33, 36
bergamot 19, 113, 117, 123
Bittered Sling 146
Blue Lightning 51
Boe, Sylvius de la 36
Booth, Felix 90
botanicals 7, 8, 14, 15, 17, 18, 23, 24, 25, 26, 28, 30, 40, 44, 52,
       66, 85, 86, 87, 88, 89, 91, 92, 93, 94, 95, 96, 97, 98, 101,
       102, 103, 104, 105, 107, 108, 109, 110, 111, 113, 114,
       115, 116, 117, 118, 121, 122, 123, 124, 125, 126, 127
Bourbon, Antoine de 35
brandewijn 36, 37
bubonic plague 16, 17
Burnett, Robert 63, 94
Burrough, James 61, 63, 69, 84, 85, 86, 103

C

D

119, 120, 121, 124
Dufour, Judith 48
Dutch Courage 42
Dutch United East Indies Company 38

E

East End 52
Elderflower Collins 145
Evans, Seager 70
excise duties 71

F

France 33, 34, 35, 42, 43, 69, 91, 97, 102, 134, 138

G

Gama, Vasco Da 13
genever 12, 33, 36, 37, 38, 39, 40, 41, 42, 44, 51, 65, 73, 84, 91,
        97, 130, 131; corenwyn 41; jonge 40, 41; korenwijn 40,
        41; oude 40, 41
Gilbey, Walter and Alfred 98
Gimlet 141
gin
   Aviation 83, 84
   Beefeater 8, 23, 61, 63, 66, 69, 84, 85, 86, 87, 103, 117, 122
   Berkeley Square 88
   Bluecoat 88, 89
   Bombay Sapphire 26, 82, 89, 90, 101
   Booth's 62, 73, 79, 90, 91
   Broker's 92
   Bulldog 93
   Burnett's White Satin 94
   Cadenhead's Old Raj 95
   Caorunn 95, 96
   Cascade Mountain Gin 96
   Citadelle Gin 97
   cold-compounded 8
   Cork Dry Gin 97

107, 108, 109, 112, 115, 119, 120, 121, 124
London Gin 7, 8, 9, 24, 25, 123
Luxembourg 33

M

Madam Geneva 46, 50, 51
maltum 53
maltwine 39, 40, 41, 130
Martinez 67, 137
Martini 76, 82, 93, 98, 106, 113, 137, 138, 139, 140, 144
Mayerne, Sir Theodore De 45
Mother Gin 50
mouth feel 30
moutwijn 39
My Lady's Eye-water 51
myrrh 40

O

orange peel 14, 23, 84, 85, 87, 91, 92, 105, 110, 112
orris 14, 23, 24, 25, 29, 87, 89, 92, 105, 107, 110, 119, 123, 124,
     126

P

Parliament 59
Parliamentary Brandy 50
Payne, Desmond 86
phylloxera 69, 85
Pimm's No 1 129, 130
pine 15, 16, 29, 118
Pink Gin 140, 141
potstills 52
Prohibition 76, 77, 78, 99

Q

Queen Gin 49

R

Rectifiers 63, 64, 120
Rectifiers' Club 63
Royal Navy 22, 71, 140, 141
Royal Poverty 51

S

saffron 19, 91, 95
Salerno 34
Savoy 74, 78
Spain 34, 42, 108, 127, 134
Stein, Robert 9
St Giles 47, 52, 54, 67, 120
stillatory 34
St John's wort 40

T

Tanqueray, Edward 64
taste
   bitter 18, 20, 23, 29, 30, 66, 67, 68, 72, 74, 90, 93, 98, 107,
        112, 113, 114, 116, 119, 120, 127, 137, 139
   salty 18, 20, 23, 29, 30, 66, 67, 68, 72, 74, 90, 93, 98, 107,
        112, 113, 114, 116, 119, 120, 127, 137, 139
   sour 18, 20, 23, 29, 30, 66, 67, 68, 72, 74, 90, 93, 98, 107,
        112, 113, 114, 116, 119, 120, 127, 137, 139
   sweet 18, 20, 23, 29, 30, 66, 67, 68, 72, 74, 90, 93, 98, 107,
        112, 113, 114, 116, 119, 120, 127, 137, 139
   umami 18, 20, 23, 29, 30, 66, 67, 68, 72, 74, 90, 93, 98, 107,
        112, 113, 114, 116, 119, 120, 127, 137, 139
The Bramble 143
The Company of Distillers 45
The Criterion 74
Thirty Years War 42
Thompson & Fearon 70
Tom Collins 67
tonic water 72, 80, 134, 135, 136
turpentine 51

V

W

Geraldine Coates writes extensively on gin and travels the country introducing people to the delights of the juniper elixir. She is also the Editor of www. gintime.com, the world's first web site devoted to gin and contributes regularly to a number of drinks publications. This is her fifth gin related book.